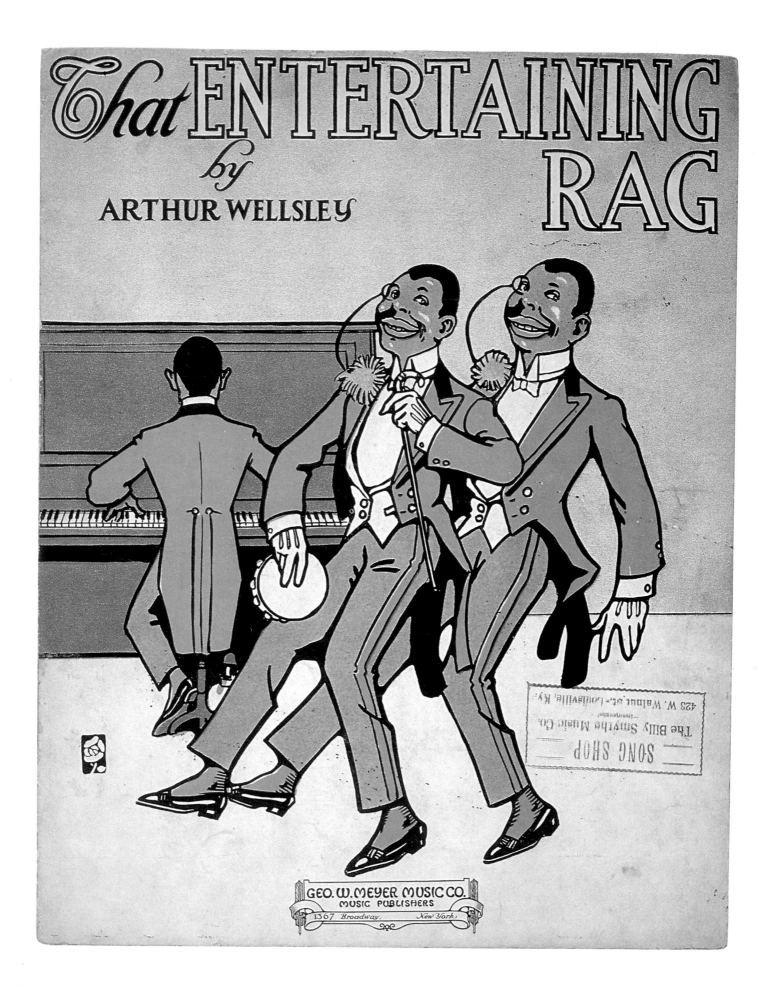

FROM CAKEWALKS TO CONCERT HALLS

An Illustrated History of African American Popular Music from 1895 to 1930

By Thomas L. Morgan
and William Barlow

ELLIOTT & CLARK PUBLISHING

Washington, D.C.

Many thanks to Hild Creed, Dorothy Morgan, Bill Magee,
Craig Schenck, Ralph and Marilyn Andresen,
Mary Alice Parsons, and Elizabeth Brown Lockman.
—T. L. M.

(Page 1) Detail from "Carnival Sketches," 1925.
(Page 2) "That Entertaining Rag," 1912.
(Page 4) Detail of Bert Williams from "The Moon
Shines on the Moonshine," 1920.

Captions and biographies by Thomas L. Morgan
Chapter text by William Barlow
Song-sheet illustrations courtesy of
Thomas L. Morgan Collection
Photographs on pages 59, 63, 70, 115, 119, and
122 courtesy of the Schomburg Center for Research
in Black Culture, New York Public Library, Astor
Lenox and Tilden Foundations; on page 112 courtesy
of the Eubie Blake National Museum, Baltimore;
on page 73 courtesy of Terry Parrish.

Designed by Gibson Parsons Design
Edited by Elizabeth Brown Lockman

Printed in Singapore through Palace Press
5 4 3 2   99 98 97 96 95 94 93

Library of Congress Cataloging-in-Publication Data
Morgan, Thomas L. (Thomas Lesher), 1952–
    From cakewalks to concert halls : an illustrated
history of African American popular music from 1895
to 1930 / by Thomas L. Morgan and William Barlow.
        p.   cm.
    Includes bibliographical references and index.
    ISBN 1-880216-17-5
    1. Afro-Americans—Music—History and criticism.
2. Popular music—United States—History and criticism.
I. Barlow, William. II. Title.
ML3479 . M67   1992
781 . 64 ' 089 ' 96073—dc20   92-8996
                                                CIP
                                                MN

TABLE OF CONTENTS

"BOBOLISHION'S COMING"

On the eve of the Emancipation Proclamation, black popular music was primarily a folk music with well-established sacred and secular oral traditions. Some 50 years later, it would be heard on the Broadway stage and Tin Pan Alley.

The religious folksongs, commonly referred to as spirituals, which were African Americans' first contribution to the popular music of the United States, began to emerge early in the 1800s. The songs tended to feature Old Testament figures and stories altered to fit the perilous situation facing the black slave population. Slaves sang about "Brudder David" triumphing over the giant Goliath, "Brudder Samson" destroying his tormentors and himself in the heathens' temple, "Brudder Joshua" bringing down the walls of Jericho, and they often alluded to the story of Moses, who freed the Hebrew slaves held captive by the wicked Old Pharaoh in Egypt.

The spirituals paid special tribute to Daniel in the lion's den, Jonah in the whale's belly, Noah on the ark, and especially Jesus on the cross; these biblical prophets were the slaves' saviors and re-deemers, just as Old Pharaoh and Old Satan were their most ominous enemies. The biblical parables they adopted in song dovetailed with their cultural paradigms of good and evil, sin and retribution, crime and punishment. In short, the spirituals were a psychological weapon in the struggle against slavery.

Antebellum spirituals, like their secular counterparts, were most often composed sponta-neously, usually to fit a specific event. Many of the themes were recycled, but they were also shaped and reshaped to reflect each individual context within a familiar cultural framework. For example, the popular spiritual:

> Go down, Moses,
> Way down in Egypt land
> Tell Old Pharaoh
> Let my people go.

was revised by a group of runaway slaves in Washington, D.C., shortly after President Lincoln issued the Emancipation Proclamation in 1863:

> Go down, Abraham,
> Away down in Dixie land
> Tell Jeff Davis
> To let my people go.

The songwriting process among slaves was often both spontaneous and collective in nature. During the Civil War, James Miller McKim, a collector of spirituals, wrote down the following conversation with a slave:

> I asked one of these blacks—one of the most intelligent I had met—where they got these songs. "Dey make em, sah." "How do they make them?" After a pause, evidently casting about for an explanation, he said, "I'll tell you; it's dis way. My master call me up and order

Before World War II, plantation life was often romanticized both on sheet music covers and in popular literature. Images of African Americans were used to sell everything from tobacco to breakfast cereal, and covers depicting blacks or suggesting black musical themes proved to enhance songs' popularity.

me a short peck of corn and a hundred lash.
My friends see it and is sorry for me. When dey
come to de praise meeting dat night dey sing
about it. Some's very good singers and know
how; and dey work it in, work it in, you know;
till dey get it right; and dat's dey way.

No more peck of corn for me
no more peck of corn
no more peck of corn for me
many thousand die.

No more hundred lash for me
no more hundred lash
no more hundred lash for me
many thousand die.

Antebellum spirituals fell into two broad categories. The first were the uptempo "shouts" or "jubilees" featuring a song leader and a chorus engaged in a call-and-response musical dialogue. Some of the most popular of these songs were "Roll Jordan Roll," "God Ring That Bell," and "In Dat Great Getting up Morning."

The slower-paced, more somber spirituals, which W. E. B. DuBois would later characterize as "sorrow songs," sprang from African lullabies and European Protestant hymns.

Based on long-phrased melodies, they usually featured solo vocalists as well as choirs. Among the best-known spirituals of this type were "Nobody Knows the Trouble I've Seen," "Motherless Child," and "Let My People Go." Thematically, these songs tended to resonate with a deep yearning for freedom from slavery and a collective vision of a brighter future—either in this world or the next.

Black secular songs in the antebellum period shared many musical traits with the spirituals, including the use of complex rhythms, gapped scales, repetition of short melodic phrases, and call-and-response singing. They also addressed the same moral and social concerns, but with more of a propensity for realism and parody. Slave seculars were most often folksongs of satire, caution, derision, or "double-voiced" praise, invariably focusing on one of slavery's innumerable grievances. For example:

The big bee flies high,
the little bee makes the honey.
The black folks make the cotton,
and the white folks gets the money.

Their origins can be traced back to West African *griots*. These musicians and storytellers were not only at the hub of their cultures, they were also the "living libraries" of the region's Bantu-language tribes, none of which had their own writing system. Another precursor was *kaiso*, an African song tradition prevalent among Bantu-speaking peoples, which dramatized right-doing and wrong-doing through the use of humorous lyrics. In the United States, this practice came to be known as putting someone "on de banjo"—be he slave or master. The subversive reversal of master/slave roles was a common ploy in those slave seculars which aspired to social satire, such as the following:

O massa take that bran' new coat
and hang it on the wall.
That darky take the same ole coat
and wear it to the ball.

Another special trait of slave folksongs was the practice of "double voicing" lyrics to ensure that black and white listeners came away with different understandings of the same song. Relating an incident which occurred in South Carolina shortly after the slaves were officially emancipated in 1865, the following white commentator, quoted in Dena J. Epstein's *Sinful Tunes and Spirituals: Black Folk Music to the Civil War*, unwittingly documented this device:

Momma and I walked slowly down the avenue to the public road, with a yelling mob of men, women and children around us. They sang, sometimes in unison, sometimes in parts, strange words which we did not understand, followed by a much-repeated chorus.

I free, I free!
I free as a frog!
I free til I fool!
Glory Alleluia!

They revolved around us, holding out their skirts and dancing now with slow, swinging movements, now with rapid jig-motions, but always with the weird chant and wild gestures.

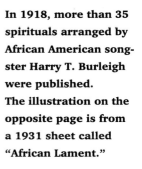

Some of these "freedom songs," like "Bobolishion's Coming" and "I Want Some Valiant Soldier," were associated with the Abolitionist movement in the North before the Civil War. But most of them seemed to have first surfaced in the wake of Lincoln's 1863 Emancipation Proclamation, freeing slaves held in the breakaway southern states, and then again in 1865, when Congress passed the 13th Amendment to the Constitution, abolishing slavery throughout the land.

The songs celebrated the end of slavery as both a historic event and a historical vehicle destined, like the legendary "Freedom Train," to carry the ex-slaves toward a better day. By the end of the Civil War and with the onset of Reconstruction, freedom songs including "No More Auction Block," "Before I'd Be a Slave," and "Let My People Go" were popular with blacks across the country.

Black popular song continued to flourish in the postbellum era, and the spirituals began to be recognized as cultural treasures. They were

In 1918, more than 35 spirituals arranged by African American songster Harry T. Burleigh were published. The illustration on the opposite page is from a 1931 sheet called "African Lament."

adopted by newly established African American churches and schools, where they became institutionalized in religious ceremonies and music curricula. With the onset of Reconstruction, spirituals were formally introduced to educated white audiences by amateur choral groups.

The most renowned of these was the Fisk Jubilee Singers from Fisk College in Nashville, Tennessee. George L. White, the white instructor who established the group, trained his student ensemble to sing the European classics, but he also encouraged them to sing "their own music." In 1871, White took the Fisk troupe on its first national tour to raise funds for the college. Their concert repertoire included patriotic anthems like the "Battle Hymn of the Republic" and sentimental minstrel ballads like "Old Folks at Home," but it also incorporated a selection of spirituals.

The Fisk Jubilee Singers were the first black vocal ensemble to introduce the African American spiritual to white audiences at home and abroad. In seven years they were able to raise $150,000 for their college—no small amount in the 1870s. Their success initiated a vocal ensemble tradition at other black colleges, which started with the Hampton Jubilee Singers, formed at Hampton College, Virginia, in 1872. As a result of performances by such choral groups, spirituals became popular with black and white audiences throughout the United States.

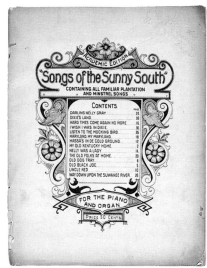

Published at the beginning of the twentieth century, this song book features compositions by Stephen Foster.

Worksongs were a vital component of black folk music for at least as long as spirituals. West African tribal societies characteristically worked to music with a strong groundbeat. All kinds of labor—building new dwellings, clearing fields, harvesting crops, preparing food, weaving cloth—were coordinated and harmonized through the use of song.

When the slaves were brought to the United States, they continued to sing variations of these songs wherever they were sold into bondage. Worksongs were heard on the cotton, sugar, and tobacco plantations, in the mines and lumber camps, and during the construction of railroads, canals, and roads. Slave owners and overseers usually encouraged their use, especially where they seemed to increase productivity and morale among the slaves.

After the Civil War, the work routines of black agricultural laborers in the South did not change a great deal in spite of their freedom, and neither did their worksongs. However, a variety of industrial occupations were now open to black laborers, and as they became stevedores, hemp spinners, turpentine workers, and furnace crewmembers on steamboats and then on the railroads, new worksongs evolved reflecting their labors. When prisons began to fill with black convicts, they also became repositories of black folk music. Due to the widespread exploitation of convict labor in the South, an injustice which would persist well into the next century, worksongs were especially prevalent behind bars.

Like spirituals, worksongs were created spontaneously; the process was extremely flexible and usually involved more than one person. The most popular worksongs, sung wherever African Americans engaged in manual labor, were well known among the general black population. Their lyrics invariably stressed oppressive work conditions, labor hardships, and poor wages, and were most often structured in a call-and-response pattern.

Worksongs enabled black workers to articulate grievances against their white bosses and drew from a deep wellspring of rage at being victimized on the basis of race. In the words of one famous example:

> *We raise the wheat*
> *Dey gib us de corn*
> *We bake de bread*
> *Dey gib us de crust*
> *We sif' de meal*
> *Dey gib us de huss*
> *We peel de meat*
> *Dey gib us de skin*
> *And dat's de way*
> *Dey take us in*
> *We skin de pot*
> *Dey gib us de liquor*
> *And say dat's good enough for de nigger*
> *Walk over, walk over*
> *Your butter and fat*
> *Poor nigger, you can't git over dat*
> *Walk over, walk over.*

Naturally enough, the best-known worksongs associated with prison life were escape epics. "Lost John," for example, told the story of a mythical black convict who eluded his captors by putting heels on the front of his shoes to match those in the back. A version of the song was transcribed as follows:

> *One day, one day*
> *I were walkin' along*
> *And I heard a little voice*
> *Didn't see no one*
> *It was old Lost John*
> *He said he was long gone*
> *Like a turkey through the corn*
> *With his long clothes on*
> *He had a heel in front*
> *And a heel behind*
> *Well you couldn't hardly tell*
> *Well you couldn't hardly tell*
> *Whichaway he was goin'*
> *Whichaway he was goin'*
> *He was long gone*
> *Long John*

Lost John was a variant of John De Conqueror, a trickster folk hero famous for outwitting his white owners during slavery. The setting of the Lost John epic was simply updated from the plantation to the prison farm; the storyline and struggle, however, remained essentially the same.

Closely related to worksongs were field

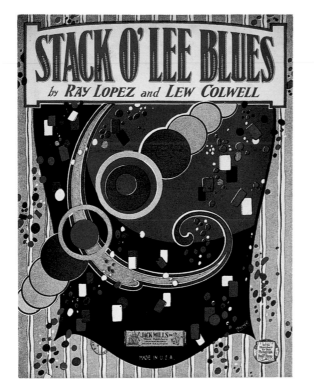

This song from 1924 is one of many written about the black anti-hero Stagolee. The most popular version, recorded by Lloyd Price in 1958, was called "Stagger Lee."

infused with African rhythms and African American folklore. Black songsters supplanted the tragic lovers and natural-disaster victims of the white tradition with a pantheon of African American folk heroes, tricksters, and outlaws.

Many of the heroes were based on historical figures. The most famous African American ballad, "John Henry," was created in honor of a black worker who died driving steel spikes for a railroad construction company in West Virginia in the early 1870s. Another African American archetype prominently featured in black ballads was the trickster. West African folklore abounds with cunning anthropomorphic animals like Ananse, the clever spider, and on North American soil, the Signifying Monkey, the indestructible Boll Weevil, and Brer Rabbit, the prankster hare from the Uncle Remus tales, came to the forefront. Black ballads also championed the outlaw figure, the stereotypical "bad nigger." As with African American folk heroes, many of these black anti-heroes were actual outlaws who perished for their misdeeds—John Hardy, Morris Slater a.k.a. "Railroad Bill," and Aaron Harris to name but a few. The following is a typical example of these characters' style of signifying:

> *I's wild nigger Bill*
> *From Redpepper Hill*
> *I never did work, an I never will*
> *I done killed de boss*
> *I's knocked down de hoss*
> *I eats up raw goose without apple sauce.*

hollers. Also called arhoolies, they were essentially a solitary field hand's vocalization of his or her identity and mood. Originally, the singer employed an African style of yodeling which stressed the use of blue notes, falsetto, and melisma. By the postbellum era, however, field hollers were not only personal signature pieces, they also began to encode verbal impressions of life in rudimentary rhyme. In this manner, they evolved into early folk blues.

A third black folksong genre prominent during the Reconstruction era and its aftermath was the African American ballad. Modeled on the traditional British ballads popular among white settlers in the Appalachian Mountains, these narratives when taken over by black music makers were

Perhaps the most infamous of these black desperados was Stagolee. Like John Henry whose legend he rivaled, Stagolee was based on a historical figure. The fact that both John Henry and Stagolee gained national recognition as folk legends suggests not only that these ballads were integral to the black popular music of the day but also that they enjoyed considerable popularity among whites as well.

Far more popular with white audiences, however, were the sentimental and comic songs of minstrelsy, a theatrical tradition which had a dramatic and sustained impact on black music throughout the nineteenth century. The roots of this unique entertainment form can be traced back to the beginnings of popular theater in the United States. Even in the late 1700s, white American actors were "blacking up" to enhance their comic imitations of African Americans on stage, and by the 1830s, black song and dance had become an integral part of this caricature.

The most famous blackface performer of the antebellum period was Thomas D. Rice, popularizer of the Jim Crow novelty act. Rice based his performance on a song and dance he learned from a crippled black stablehand on his travels in the South. One account claims that he even borrowed the old stablehand's ragged clothing for the routine's premiere. In any event, the Jim Crow skit was a smashing success. Rice toured the major theaters in the United States and then England as a star attraction. In the process, his new trademark song, "Jump Jim Crow," also called "Zip Coon," became one of the most popular minstrel numbers of the era.

In its pre-Civil War heyday, blackface minstrelsy evolved into a thriving entertainment business. Minstrel shows became famous for stage extravaganzas requiring numerous performers, elaborate costumes, and an army of supporting cast and technicians.

Stephen Foster was the most talented songwriter working in minstrelsy during this period; his sentimental ballads, especially "Old Black Joe," "Old Folks at Home," and "My Old Kentucky Home," became classics of American popular song. Another major blackface minstrel star of the time was E. P. Christy, whose troupe established the standard minstrel show format. It included a set progression of skits and songs, as well as a set number of performers with well-defined roles, like the comic end men, Mr. Tambo and Mr. Bones, and the master of ceremonies, Mr. Interlocutor.

Blackface minstrels quickly attracted a large and enthusiastic working-class following in both the North and the South. Their comic portrayal of African Americans as childlike and contented slaves tended to reinforce the prejudices of their audiences. By reassuring whites that African Americans were

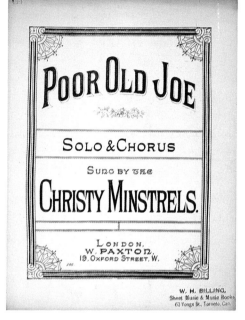

The Christy Minstrels used this 1885 song in one of their blackface routines.

George M. Cohan was one of many performers who got their show business start in minstrel shows. The first minstrel group, The Virginia Minstrels, consisted of four men. By the turn of the century, the shows boasted large casts. An example is George "Honey Boy" Evans and His Hundred Honey Boys, a troupe featured on many sheet music covers including "The Memphis Blues."

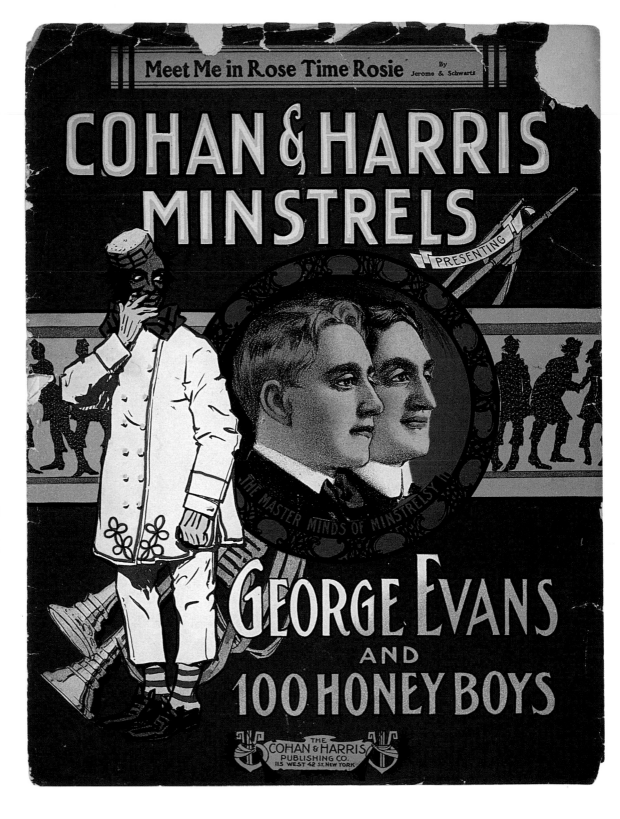

at least a step below them on the biological ladder, blackface minstrel stereotypes helped support the notion that slavery was a justifiable form of paternalism.

After the Civil War, when black minstrels began to perform in public, they forced many of their white imitators to look for another stage gimmick. However, the business affairs of minstrelsy remained firmly in the hands of white entrepreneurs who continued to own, control, and profit from the major minstrel shows. They also insisted that the black minstrels working for them remain faithful to the antebellum blackface tradition. Hence, in order to secure gainful employment, many African American entertainers adopted the stereotyped characters and routines of blackface minstrelsy, including, paradoxically, the custom of blacking up. Although they did manage to infuse these caricatures with authentic folk songs, dances, and humor from their own culture, over the next few decades the compromises black entertainers had to make yielded mixed results.

The career of James Bland vividly illustrates some of the artistic ironics and frustrations inherent in black minstrelsy. Born into a middle-class black family, he spent his youth in Washington, D.C., and there attended Howard University before going into minstrelsy. During his tenure as the most famous black minstrel songwriter of the postbellum era, Bland wrote more than 700 songs, most of which were sentimental ballads or jubilee-style spirituals. Early in his minstrel career, Bland performed a "refined comedy" routine in blackface, and his songs were replete with stereotypical, idealized plantation imagery. His best-known composition, "Carry Me Back to Old Virginny," about a freed slave longing for his former master and the good old plantation life during slavery became the state anthem of Virginia.

After enjoying a period of minstrel stardom in the 1870s, Bland spent most of the next decade touring in Europe, where he could perform without blacking up. While in Europe, he matured as both a performer and a composer. Unfortunately, when he finally returned to the United States in the 1890s, his days as a minstrel star were long forgotten. In spite of his European triumphs, Bland was not able to make a comeback on North American soil. There was no work for a cultured and serious black minstrel. He dropped out of the public eye, and years later died in impoverished obscurity in Philadelphia, Pennsylvania.

The most popular black minstrel star of the postbellum period was Billy Kersands. In his heyday in the 1870s and 1880s, he was the highest-paid African American entertainer in minstrelsy, making up to $100 a week. Although his many business ventures into the independent ownership and production of minstrel troupes proved fruitless, Kersands still managed to remain the nominal

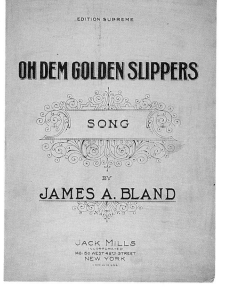

This is a 1928 copy of one of James Bland's most popular songs.

leader of his own troupe throughout most of his career. In fact, he often traveled with his own marching brass band, which enjoyed a national reputation for excellence.

On stage, however, Kersands played a slow-witted buffoon, a stereotypical role reinforced by his unusually large mouth and lips, which he highlighted with blackface. He liked to amaze people by placing a cup and saucer inside his mouth, and included this stunt in his stage act. Yet Kersands was also a talented dancer who may well have been the originator of soft-shoe dancing. In addition, he was a skillful interpreter of black folklore with an exceptional ability to mask his voice in a number of vocal disguises through the use of dialects. In his most famous songs, Kersands became alternately the frogs and the crows, or took on the persona of Old Aunt Jemima to dramatize a fable about the promise and the reality of freedom in the postbellum era. Hence, his stage act had something in it for everybody—from the white owners who feasted on its profits and the white audiences who laughed at its stereotypes to the African American audiences who flocked to his shows in great numbers to witness his dancing and singing, as well as his double-voiced humor and parody.

One of the more unsavory musical trends to which Billy Kersands may have inadvertently contributed was the emergence of the infamous "coon song" as a staple of black minstrelsy. The characterization of humorous minstrel novelty tunes as coon songs originated in the antebellum era in conjunction with the rising popularity of the "Zip Coon" stereotype, a black urban dandy vainly trying to imitate the mannerisms of his former masters. The caricature and accompanying songs were first popularized by blackface minstrel George Washington Dixon in the 1830s. They were then taken over by black minstrels like Kersands, whose best-known coon song, "Mary's Gone with a Coon," was actually a self-parody of the African American stigma associated with darker skin pigmentation.

These songs of racial mockery continued to flourish in postbellum black minstrelsy. During the 1890s, they reached their zenith—or nadir—with the publication of Ernest Hogan's "All Coons Look Alike to Me." Although the actual lyrics were inane, the title struck a responsive chord, both with the public at large and the entertainment industry. Almost single-handedly, the song was responsible for bringing the old minstrel stereotypes back to the Broadway stage, and then on to Tin Pan Alley.

Even though black minstrelsy persisted well into the 1920s, its heyday came before the turn of the century. The two white showmen who dominated the minstrel enterprise during this period were Charles Callender and J. H. Haverly. Their various troupes were renowned for presenting the most lavish black minstrel shows of the day. Along with numerous other lesser-known and shorter-lived troupes, they made seasonal tours of the rural South, visiting the cotton belt in the fall and the tobacco belt in the spring. They also played in

The most famous coon song is credited to Ernest Hogan, a black man both surprised and troubled by the way his composition was received. It was originally called "All Pimps Look Alike to Me," and when Bob Cole and Rosamond Johnson performed the song, they substituted "boys" for "coons." At one 1900 ragtime contest, all the piano players who reached the semifinals were weeded out by having to rag two minutes of this song.

Coon songs were billed as authentic black music, and indeed some of the phrases and musical elements were based on African American folk tradition. The lyrics often focused on jamborees or the gastronomical delights of chicken, pork chops, and watermelon. In the songs, most of the women were red-hot, most of the men were unfaithful, and a straight razor solved most disputes.

18

small mill towns, lumber and levee camps, and increasingly in theaters in large urban centers. The major black troupes toured in special cars and performed under large canvas tents when no theater halls were readily available. They were made up of musicians, comics, singers, dancers, novelty acts, and a work crew hired to take care of the portable stage, seating, tent, and equipment.

Because black minstrelsy was the first African American foothold in mainstream show business, it established norms that were carried over into later enterprises in those sectors of the entertainment industry catering to black artists and audiences: in particular, the race record labels, the music publishing firms in New York, and the urban vaudeville theater circuits. Some of the most esteemed black performers who got their start in postbellum minstrelsy included Sam Lucas, Bert Williams, W. C. Handy, Ma Rainey, and Bessie Smith.

In many ways, Sam Lucas was the most multifaceted of the great black minstrel performers. His career spanned almost five decades: from 1869, the year he broke into minstrelsy at age 19, to 1915, the year he became the first black male cast in a major film role.

On stage Lucas, who was born in Ohio to free black parents, played the obligatory comedy roles, but he also sang his own songs. Many of his most popular compositions, like "Emancipation Day," "De Day I Was Sot Free," and "My Dear Old Southern Home," celebrated the end of slavery.

Although they were written in the standard sentimental ballad style popularized by Stephen Foster and James Bland, their sentiments were hardly an endorsement of antebellum plantation life:

> *I remember now my poor wife's face*
> *her cries ring in my ear.*
> *When they tore me from her wild embrace*
> *and sold me way out here.*
> *My children sobbed about my knees*
> *they're all grown up since then*
> *But bless de Lord de good times come*
> *I'se freed by dose Northern men.*

Lucas was never content with the constraints inherent in minstrel comedy. He habitually sought out serious acting roles and projects. For a time, he teamed up with the famous black actresses, the Hyer Sisters, to stage two musical dramas, *The Underground Railroad* and *Out of Bondage*. Later in his career, he became the first black actor to play the title role in a serious stage production of *Uncle Tom's Cabin*. In the 1890s, Lucas was also in the forefront of transforming black minstrelsy into black musical theater. He starred in one of the first New York black musical revues, "The Creole Show," in 1890, and he also took part in *A Trip to Coontown*, which is often referred to as the first black musical, later in the decade. In addition, he performed in two of Cole and Johnson's early black musicals, *The Shoo-fly Regiment* and *Red Moon*. Lucas then topped off his prolific career

Topsy was a character in Harriet Beecher Stowe's abolitionist novel, *Uncle Tom's Cabin*. When the best-selling book was adapted to the stage, it was one of only a handful of nineteenth-century plays in which black actors were allowed to practice their craft. Even so, before the turn of the century, the title character, Uncle Tom, was always played by a white man in blackface.

TOPSY

TWO-STEP

BY
LIBBIE ERICKSON

5

W.C.Polla Company
PUBLISHERS.
GRAND OPERA HOUSE BLOCK.
CHICAGO. U. S.A.

by playing the lead in the silent film version of *Uncle Tom's Cabin*.

Lucas was undoubtedly the greatest black actor of his era, a pioneer who helped bridge the gap between black minstrelsy and black musical theater. This transition unshackled African American popular music from the legacy of blackface minstrelsy and ushered in an extraordinary renaissance in black popular song.

The last two decades of the nineteenth century saw a black musical reawakening in the South, launched by the first generation of African Americans born after slavery. During that 20-year span, no less than three distinct yet overlapping genres of black popular music blossomed: ragtime, blues, and jazz. Their sudden flowering radically transformed not only black popular song, but mainstream American popular music in general. Ragtime, perhaps the oldest of the three, was eventually · absorbed by jazz. Blues and jazz, on the other hand, continued to be major influences on popular song in the United States throughout the twentieth century.

The roots of ragtime can be traced back to the practice of "ragging" European dance music, a technique developed by slave musicians in the antebellum South. Playing banjos, fiddles, and an assortment of homemade rhythm makers in small ensembles, they would overlay the basic rhythmic and/or melodic structures of European songs with alternative rhythmic schemes. This was accomplished by two or more musicians playing the competing rhythmic patterns simultaneously, or by one musician on a string instrument playing a separate pattern with each hand or with different finger and thumb combinations to achieve the desired cross rhythms. This polyrhythmic principle has always been prominently featured in the drumming traditions of West Africa, and the practice indeed may have come from there.

By the postbellum era, ragging a tune was being called "syncopation" in educated music circles and being highlighted in the dance numbers staged by black minstrel troupes. They not only popularized this new musical trend, they also created new dance routines, like Billy Kersands' trademark buck and wing, to go along with certain songs.

The piano slowly emerged as the instrument favored by most black musicians intent on experimenting with ragging their music. Undoubtedly, the best-known pioneer of this form was Scott Joplin. Joplin was born into a musical family and grew up in East Texas after the Civil War. He was a child prodigy on the piano, and while still a teenager, he migrated to St. Louis to pursue a musical career. St. Louis at the time was a thriving river port and railroad center with a prosperous red-light district. Consequently, it was also a hotbed for black musicians seeking employment in its saloons, nightclubs, brothels, dance halls, and theaters.

Joplin first found work as a pianist at

"Maple Leaf" was Scott Joplin's best-selling song; this cover, though published at the turn of the century, is not a first edition.

Published by Scott Joplin in 1908, this extremely rare sheet music cover contains piano exercises intended to help students understand Joplin's approach to ragtime.

"Honest" John Turpin's Silver Dollar Saloon. Turpin was a rough-and-tumble black entrepreneur famous for his feats as a professional fighter who specialized in head butting, and his saloon was a haven for young black pianists experimenting with ragtime. Turpin's son Tom, who was Joplin's age, was himself an aspiring piano player and composer, and the two struck up a close musical friendship.

Tom Turpin left St. Louis in the late 1880s to prospect for gold in the Rocky Mountains, but he returned in the early 1890s and opened the Rosebud Cafe, complete with gambling facilities, an upstairs bordello, and a downstairs saloon where such up-and-coming ragtime pianists as Scott Joplin, Joe Jordan, Sam Patterson, Charles Hunter, and Louis Chauvin played. Renewing his friendship with Joplin, Turpin continued his experimentation with ragtime piano music and published his first composition, "Harlem Rag."

By the late 1890s, Scott Joplin had moved on to Sedalia, Missouri. There he published his most famous composition, "Maple Leaf Rag." Named after a local social club where Joplin often played, the song became the biggest instrumental ragtime hit of the era, selling more than one million copies of sheet music.

It was also in Sedalia that Joplin initiated his highly productive relationship with music publisher John Stark, who not only published his music, but also helped finance the rest of his career. After the turn of the century, Joplin moved to New York City where he published his own ragtime instruction book called *School of Ragtime*. Later in his life, he endeavored to write more serious and elaborate compositions and even folk operas until he finally succumbed to the ravages of syphilis in 1917.

Between 1880 and 1900, the tenderloins of a number of cities besides Saint Louis hosted budding ragtime milieus, including New Orleans, Memphis, Kansas City, Chicago, Baltimore, Philadelphia, and New York. New Orleans was home base for the legendary John Baptist, a ragtime pianist whose playing style dominated the local music scene in the 1870s and 1880s. He was superseded in the 1890s by Tony Jackson, a gifted young songwriter who was also credited with being the father of the left-handed walking bass ragtime and blues piano riff. His close friend, Ferdinand "Jelly Roll" Morton was a pivotal figure in New Orleans ragtime and jazz, especially after the turn of the century.

During this period, Memphis had a lively red-light district located along Beale Street and a trio of homegrown ragtime piano legends: Hatchett, Bad Hooks, and Willie Bloom. Kansas City was home to Otis Saunders, who had spent time with his good friend Scott Joplin in Sedalia; and James Scott, the second-most famous ragtime composer of the day after Joplin.

Chicago's ragtime fans boasted about Johnny Seymore and "Pluck" Henry, a ragtime banjo virtuoso who transformed his unique banjo

Scott Joplin, born in Texas in 1868, became famous as a composer of classic rags in 1899, when John Stark of Missouri published his "Maple Leaf Rag." The song eventually sold over a million copies. "Nonpareil," published in 1907 and his twentieth composition, was never copyrighted. Although Joplin was an accomplished composer, he shied away from public performances later in his career because he did not consider himself a strong piano player.

There are several different theories about the origin of the term "rag." Some say it stems from an 1899 reference to African American clog dancing as "ragging;" others trace it to a dance which featured interaction between participants and spectators and was known as a "rag." A third and more poetic explanation is that adding syncopation to a song metaphorically tears it to pieces. Rags like this 1909 publication are known for their colorful covers.

picking style to the piano. Black musicians based in Baltimore, Philadelphia, Boston, and New York City developed a unique style of ragtime piano which drew on Cuban habanera rhythms and Geechie ring shouts, a religious song-and-dance folk ritual popular among African Americans from the southern Atlantic lowlands. The best-remembered of the first-generation ragtime piano giants from this region included William Turk and Sammy Ewell in Baltimore, Sam Moore and "No Legs" Cagey in Philadelphia, "One Leg" Willie Joseph in Boston, and Sam Gordon, Jess Picket, Richard McLean a.k.a. Abba Labba, and Jack the Bear in New York City.

The minstrel songwriter and performer most responsible for popularizing ragtime as a national musical fad was Ben Harney, the self-proclaimed "Inventor of Ragtime." Harney was born near Middleboro, Kentucky, in 1871, and he began his career in minstrelsy as a teenager in nearby Louisville. Two of his first compositions, "You've Been a Good Old Wagon" and "Mister Johnson Turn Me Loose," both published in the mid-1890s, demonstrated his early attraction to ragtime and the blues respectively.

Harney's big break came in 1896, when he performed his ragtime numbers at the renowned Tony Pastor's Music Hall in New York City. The appearance was a triumph. Ragtime soon became the rage of Broadway and Tin Pan Alley, and Harney went on to become one of the most popular ragtime performers of the era. His predilection for

black music and culture and the fact that he often performed with black entertainers have spurred an ongoing debate among music historians about Harney's racial identity. He claimed that his parents were white, and he married a white woman, but many of his black contemporaries believed that he was only passing for white to further his show business career. Whatever the case, Ben Harney had a real affinity for ragtime.

In an interview later in his life, he spoke of the origins of his favorite music with authority and insight:

Real ragtime on piano, played in such a manner that it cannot be put in notes, is the contribution of the graduated Negro banjo player who cannot read music. On the banjo there is a short string that is not fretted and that consequently is played upon with the thumb. It is frequently referred to as the thumb string. The colored performer, strumming in his own cajoling way, likes to throw in a note at random, and his thumb ranges over the string for this effect. When he takes up the piano, the desire for the same effect dominates him, being almost second nature, and he reaches for the open string note with his little finger. Meanwhile, he is keeping mechanically perfect time with his left hand. The hurdle with the right hand little finger throws the tune off its stride, resulting in syncopation. He is playing two different tunes at once.

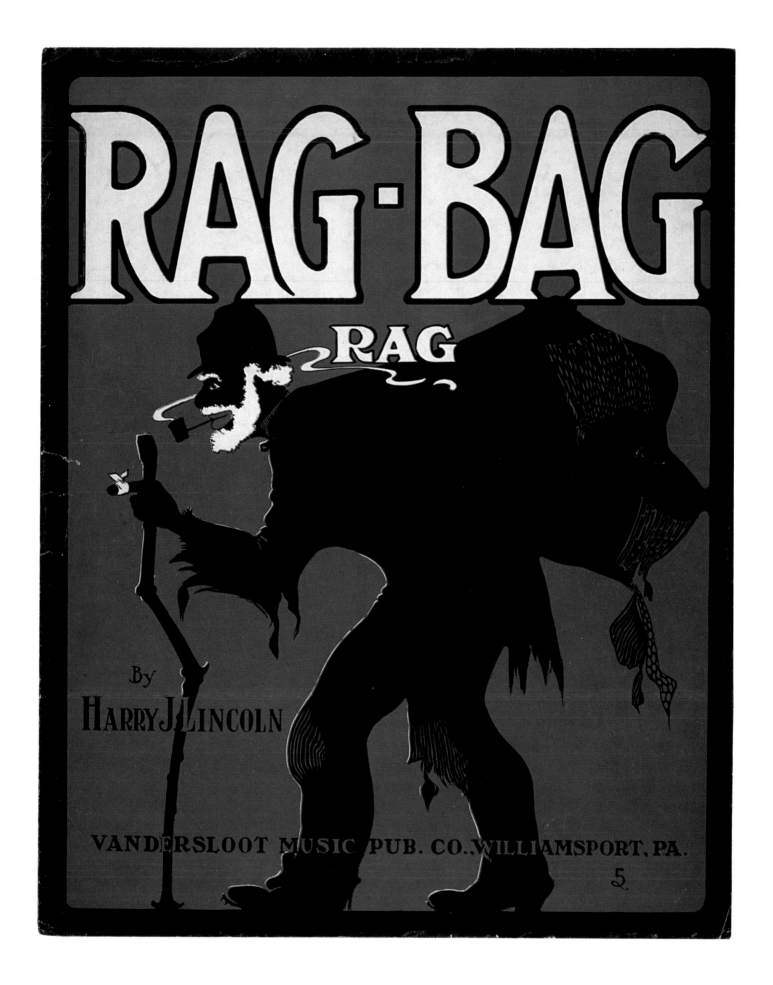

Detail of a cakewalking couple from "Eli Green's Cakewalk," 1896.

Ragtime's commercial popularity in the 1890s was accented by the arrival of the cakewalk on the New York scene. The cakewalk originated as a slave dance contest in the antebellum South. White slave owners were fond of awarding cakes to the best slave dancers at special social gatherings. The slaves themselves, however, were developing their dancing into a parody of the mannerisms and fashions of the white southern social elite. Couples dressed in their finest clothes would lean back and perform a high-stepping promenade. These slave dance routines were then expropriated by blackface minstrels and used at the end of their stage shows.

After the Civil War, black minstrels continued the tradition of staging the cakewalk as the grand finale of their performances. By the 1890s, the dance was so popular that a national Cakewalk Jubilee was held in New York City, and a number of new black musical revues included the dance as a major attraction in their shows.

Ben Harney's "Cakewalk in the Sky" was a typical cakewalk song from this period. The chorus to the tune was standard coon song fare, but Harney often sang it in Geechie dialect, which must have confused his white audiences as much as it delighted his black ones. The white English version of the chorus was as follows:

> *Put a smile on each face*
> *Every coon now take your place*
> *And then away they went*
> *All on pleasure bent*

> *The harps were ringing*
> *In ragtime they were singing*
> *And they all bowed down to the*
>   *king of coons*
> *Who taught the cakewalk in the sky.*

Ragtime's complex historical legacy was perhaps a major reason for its widespread appeal among both blacks and whites. First and foremost, it was a dance music which drew on both European and African traditions. Second, ragtime was a style grounded in an ongoing, cross-cultural, racial parody: the slaves' parody of their masters, blackface minstrels' trope of the slaves' parody, black minstrels' trope of the blackface parody, and so on. In addition, ragtime was a rural folk music transposed to an urban and industrial context, where its machine-like rhythms became an expression of the lost innocence of bygone days and ways. And finally, as a novel popular music created by the first generation of African Americans born after slavery, ragtime represented an affirmation of their newly experienced freedoms and an optimistic vision of the future. Ironically, it became a national phenomenon at approximately the same time that the progressive social reforms of the Reconstruction era virtually collapsed, and much of the country reverted back to racial policies based on the social segregation and political disenfranchisement of African Americans.

The blues emerged as a unique musical genre among black agricultural workers in the rural South during the 1890s, a bit later than ragtime. Over the next 30 years, this new music spread along with a rising tide of African American migrants to urban centers in the South and North. There the rural blues were transformed, both stylistically and lyrically, to better express the grim realities of urban living.

From their inception, the blues have been characterized by a twelve-bar, three-line (AAB) stanza structure, with the second line usually being a repetition of the first line, and the third line a response to them both. Complementing the stanza's vocal line was at least one musical accompaniment, most often a guitar. This both established the basic beat and the chord progressions and responded to the vocal lines in a call-and-response pattern. Although the twelve-bar blues became standard, the length of the blues stanza could, and often did, vary, especially in the genre's formative years.

The musical sources of the blues can be found in black field hollers, worksongs, and ballads, all of which were popular in the rural South during the post-Reconstruction era. The field hollers, in particular, always employed blue notes in their descending vocal lines. Although these "bent" or "flattened" notes were sung in between the major and minor keys of the European diatonic scale, they were more musically attuned to the African pentatonic scale. Along with the use of cross rhythms, they were the major musical innovation in early blues music. The fusion of these three folksong genres led to the birth of distinctive blues

styles and repertoires in at least three discernable regions of the rural South—the Mississippi Delta, East Texas, and the Piedmont.

The Mississippi Delta is located in the heart of the soil-rich farmlands spreading out on both sides of the Mississippi River between Natchez, Mississippi, and Memphis, Tennessee. After the Civil War, the region's white plantation owners turned from slave labor to sharecropping and tenant farming, which enabled them to reap large profits while keeping their black field hands in economic servitude. By the 1890s, the Delta had the most concentrated African American population in the entire country: blacks outnumbered whites almost four to one. The economic peonage inherent in the sharecropping and tenant farming system, the rigid Jim Crow legal system, and the lynch rope were all used to keep the large black workforce segregated, dependant on their white landlords, and resigned to their second-class status. This was the historical situation out of which the

Detail of field hands and a banjo player from "A Hot Time in the Old Town Tonight," 1896.

27

Tin Pan Alley song-writers recognized that the name "blues" would appeal to the ordinary person even if the unfamiliar musical structure of these songs might not, and so they wrote standard ballads and simply added "blues" to the titles. Hundreds of such "blues" tunes were released during the teens and twenties.

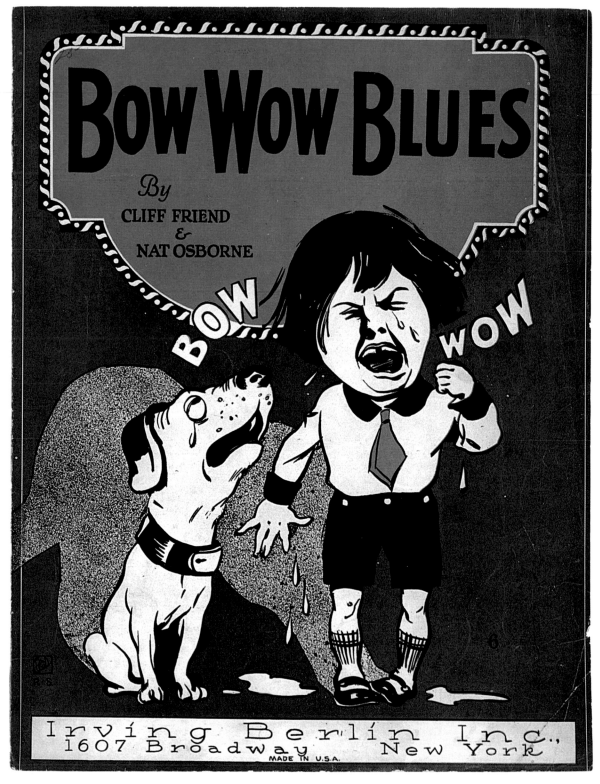

earliest Delta blues emerged. In many respects, they were a defiant response to the oppressive socio-economic conditions facing their black creators.

Blues in the Delta may have originated in the cotton fields, as many of the early musicians claimed, but they soon became the centerpiece of black recreational life. At weekend house parties, they supplemented traditional country dance music; guitars and harmonicas took the place of banjos and fiddles. In the barrelhouses and juke joints, blues joined ragtime as the music of choice among itinerant piano players.

The earliest Delta blues pioneers were field hands whose musical activities were often secondary to their cotton farming. They played on weekends and holidays for free food, drinks, and tips at local house parties and other social events. By performing in front of friends and neighbors, they were able to develop their repertoires and playing styles in a supportive environment.

The second generation of Delta blues musicians, born between 1880 and 1900, consolidated the budding tradition and eventually introduced it to a national audience. The best known of these bluesmen were Charley Patton, Son House, Tommy Johnson, and Skip James. Their blues featured two contrasting vocal styles: the rough, guttural, declamatory shouts of Charley Patton, and the tormented, introspective falsetto of Skip James. The most prominent guitar playing styles associated with the Delta blues involved the use of intense chord progressions building toward a droning crescendo, and the use of a slider, such as a bottleneck worn over a finger, to create a poignant crying sound similar to the human voice. The Delta blues tradition continued to thrive into the early decades of the twentieth century, and proved to be a source of material and inspiration for the formation of an urban blues tradition in the Midwest.

Like the Mississippi Delta, East Texas was a cotton-producing region tied to the South's plantation economy. As slavery's last refuge in the waning days of the Confederacy, the Lone Star state took in a sizable black slave population in order to keep them in bondage as long as possible. After they were finally released, most former slaves had no choice but to continue to work in the East Texas cotton fields as sharecroppers and tenant farmers. However, their populations were not as concentrated as those of their Delta counterparts due to the region's poor soil and the availability of land to the west.

The exception to this situation was along the Trinity and Brazos rivers, where the topsoil was rich and thick. These riverlands were the site not only of the state's most prosperous cotton plantations, but also of the South's most notorious prison farms. Worksongs sung by black prisoners on these prison farms proved to be a motherlode for the East Texas blues tradition, and a number of them were incorporated into the repertoires of the area's early blues players.

One of the region's best-known blues pioneers, "Ragtime Texas" Henry Thomas, was noted for his many railroad blues and prison worksongs.

He was born in 1874, the son of former slaves; his colorful career as a railroad hobo and itinerant blues musician spanned four decades, enabling him to be recorded commercially in the 1920s. In his wake, a younger group of East Texas bluesmen, including the legendary Blind Lemon Jefferson and Huddie "Leadbelly" Ledbetter, established a distinct regional style and repertoire which they would eventually popularize throughout the country.

Largest of the three rural blues homelands, the Piedmont stretches from Richmond, Virginia, south to Atlanta, Georgia. The area from Richmond down to Durham, North Carolina, and then west to the Appalachian Mountains has historically been tobacco country; farther south, cotton was king. As in the other two regions, black agricultural workers were the source and inspiration of the Piedmont blues, which seem to have emerged almost a decade after their initial documentation in East Texas and the Mississippi Delta.

The Piedmont sound was sweet, light, and fluid, a dramatic departure from the deeper and darker Delta blues, or the more jazz-influenced sound that came to the forefront in East Texas. Piedmont blues musicians favored lilting melodies sung in high, plaintive voices. They drew their material from secular folksongs, ballads, and popular standards performed by black minstrels, who had a large following in the region. In addition, early Piedmont blues innovators like Blind Arthur Blake incorporated ragtime techniques into their guitar playing, ragging blues melodies to create the desired cross rhythms. Their ragtime-influenced style stressed finger-picking dexterity and came to dominate the Piedmont blues sound.

Another musical trait of the region was the guitar and harmonica duos which flourished in the northern parts of the Piedmont. They featured intricate, interchangeable, and often overlapping call-and-response patterns. Unlike the Delta and East Texas traditions, however, the Piedmont blues never found an equivalent urban sound. As a result, they never really caught on in Eastern Seaboard cities with large black migrant populations like Washington, D.C., Philadelphia, and New York. Nonetheless, the Piedmont blues, along with its counterparts in East Texas and the Mississippi Delta, had a major impact on black popular song up until the 1930s.

In jazz, as in ragtime and blues, separating the melody from the groundbeat that ostensibly supports it enabled the free play of improvisation where it once was severely restricted. Released, the melody seems to float about the groundbeat, generating both movement and tension within the song. This essential characteristic of jazz, usually called "swing," is closely akin to the practice of ragging or syncopation.

A second essential ingredient in the making of jazz is timbre. Because West African languages come from oral traditions, and in fact have neither alphabets nor writing systems, tonality has always played a central role in their use and development. The meaning of words can alter with the slightest change of pitch. Although these languages failed, for the most part, to survive the ordeal of slavery in the United States, their propensity for sophisticated tonal coloring was passed on culturally, much to the benefit of jazz.

The early jazz pioneers developed techniques to coarsen the "sweet"-sounding timbres of the era's popular music, which was still dominated by white European standards. Two of the most common coarsening techniques were the use of blue notes and vibrato in both vocal and instrumental practices.

Most evidence points to New Orleans as the birthplace of jazz. The birth took place sometime during the 1890s. However, the rhythmic foundations of jazz can be traced back to the African drum ensembles which performed on New Orleans' Congo Square, a large public field where black slaves were allowed to assemble on Sundays to engage in traditional African songs and dances. Large drum ensembles were always a prominent aspect of these festivities, which originated prior to 1800 and continued up until just before the Civil War. The playing of drums by slaves was outlawed in the rest of the South due to the widespread fear that they would be used to convey secret messages. As the only locale where African drumming traditions were tolerated, New Orleans was the only place they survived. These polyrhythmic practices in turn played a central role in the postbellum popular music of the city's black population.

Throughout the nineteenth century, New Orleans was the nation's foremost city of pleasure. Its French beginnings, coupled with Spanish, Creole, and African American influences, set it apart from the Anglo-American cultural norms and mores that prevailed in the rest of the United States. By the 1850s, New Orleans was the largest city in the South, famous for its elegant French opera house, its sumptuous bordellos, and its quadroon balls at which beautiful young octoroon women were chosen as mistresses by the city's white male aristocracy.

The aftermath of the Civil War brought major changes to New Orleans. The city's slaveholding upper class lost most of its wealth, and a new power elite emerged in the red-light district. Italian and Irish underworld gangs now vied for control over the tenderloin's lucrative vice operations, and their ascendancy totally changed its locale and orientation. The section of New Orleans known as the French Quarter became the new center of the city's nightlife and vice.

Traditionally, the French Quarter had been populated by a free mulatto Creole caste that enjoyed a degree of prosperity before the Civil War. After the war, however, these Creoles of color lost their special status due to the African blood in their veins, and they were subjected to the same Jim Crow restrictions imposed on the former slaves. As the French Quarter consequently declined socially and economically, it was increasingly populated by foreign immigrants and rural black migrants. By the 1880s, the French Quarter was the poorest and most densely populated section of

Written in 1908, this song became a Dixieland standard, and for many years, it was performed by the same brass bands which gave a number of jazz pioneers their musical start. This particular song was used as the theme for the King of the Zulus Parade, the famous African American procession that still marks the climax of New Orleans' Mardi Gras celebration.

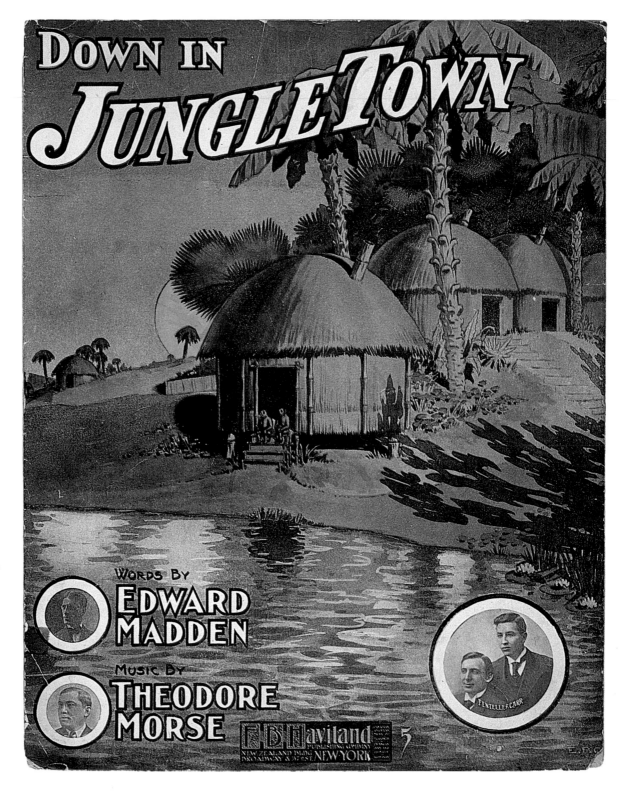

the city; as a result, its vice operations took on a lower class character.

During the postbellum period, African Americans in New Orleans organized more than 200 clubs and benevolent societies. At first, they were politically oriented, but in the wake of the Reconstruction era, the clubs' social function became their primary concern. One of their most important activities was the formation of marching brass bands. Due to its French origins, the city had always had a flair for marching bands and colorful parades. When African Americans took over these local traditions, they reoriented them to better mesh with their own social needs.

From their inception, the black brass marching bands were multifaceted: they performed at parades, picnics, park concerts, fish fries, lawn parties, political rallies, and funerals. Their music was a gumbo of European and African traditions. The brass and reed instruments were European, while most of the bands' rhythmic patterns were African in origin. They played popular martial music, traditional spirituals, and minstrel favorites, all with a ragtime flavor. These brass marching bands proved to be the street music conservatories for many of New Orleans' greatest first-generation jazz pioneers.

In the last two decades of the 1800s, the prosperity generated by New Orleans' resurgence as a trade and transportation center fueled business in the tenderloin. But social tensions were also exacerbated by a rising level of crime, violence, and ethnic conflict. Moreover, the city fathers' attempts to contain the red-light district culminated in the establishment of the famous Storyville vice zone on the west side of the French Quarter in 1897. Because of the abundance of brothels there, aspiring black piano players flocked to New Orleans during this period. Nowhere in the country, except perhaps St. Louis, was there a larger and more creative ragtime piano milieu. A few of these pianists, like Jelly Roll Morton, had an important influence on the birth of jazz. According to Morton:

All these people played ragtime in a hot style, but man you can play hot all you want, and you still won't be playing jazz. Hot means something spicey. Ragtime is a certain type of syncopation and only certain tunes can be played in that idea. But jazz is a style that can be applied to any type of tune.

One essential jazz ingredient cited by Jelly Roll Morton was what he called "Spanish tinges." These were, in realty, Cuban habanera rhythms finding their way to North American via New Orleans, and, as he declared, "If you can't manage to put tinges of Spanish in your tunes, you will never be able to get the right seasoning, I call it, for jazz."

While the ragtime pianists and marching brass bands both played key roles in the evolution of jazz in New Orleans, it was the local dance bands that actually gave birth to this new musical genre. Some of the city's dance bands evolved from marching brass bands, like the dance orchestra of John Robichoux which developed out of the Excelsior Brass Band in 1893. Robichoux was a colored Creole whose band was a favorite attraction at the dances held in Lincoln Park, the city's premier black music venue. The orchestra, which included small brass and reed sections, played the popular dance music of the era in a style local musicians referred to as "sweet."

Other, smaller bands evolved from traditional rural string bands and usually played for fish fries and lawn parties. Initially, they were made up of string instruments and harmonicas, but by the 1890s, it was not unusual for these bands to also include brass and reed instruments. Charles Galloway, a guitarist, was the leader of one of New Orleans' best-known string bands, which provided an early forum for the founding father of New Orleans jazz, Charles "Buddy" Bolden.

A New Orleans native, Buddy Bolden began his musical ascendancy while still a teenager, when he joined Galloway's band as its cornet player in the mid-1890s. His natural talent soon won him a leadership position in the group, which quickly evolved into one of the city's most sought-after dance bands. Bolden's cornet style was unique for its time; he played by ear the music he heard all around him, creating a new fusion of ragtime, brass band martial music, spirituals, and rural blues. His playing style has been described as "low down," "wide open," "rough," and especially "loud." Legend had it that his horn could be heard as far as ten miles away. Many New Orleans musicians recalled his famous "cutting contests" with John Robichoux's band in the local parks. In these musical competitions, Bolden's loud, coarse blues numbers usually carried the day, drawing the crowds away from Robichoux's sweeter-sounding dance band. By the turn of the century, Buddy Bolden was the undisputed king of New Orleans' new-sounding dance music, which was beginning to be referred to as jazz.

The prominent role vocals played in Buddy Bolden's band suggests that New Orleans jazz was far from being exclusively instrumental in its earliest manifestations. In fact, Bolden's most important musical innovation was to reorganize the city's small dance ensembles to better accommodate the blues, vocals included. This was accomplished by combining elements from the string and marching bands into a loosely structured dance-oriented unit. The string instruments—bass fiddle, guitar, and banjo—became the rhythm section, while the frontline instruments—clarinets, trombones, and cornets—improvised with the melody. By situating the blues at the center of this musical experiment, Bolden paved the way for other musicians to explore the blues form and sound. The net result was the creation of New Orleans jazz. In the next two decades, the jazz style and genre Bolden had pioneered in New Orleans would spread throughout the country as one of the new century's most exciting popular musics. Along with ragtime and the blues, it would go on to alter the soundscape of American music.

"Jazz baby" was a slang term for a sexually accessible woman; "jazz hound" described the men who craved these "babies." There are many stories about the roots of the word "jazz." Originally used in a derogatory way, the term lost its negative connotations and found its way into many song titles prior to 1920, including "Cleopatra Had a Jazz Band," "The Jazz Dance," "Jazzola," "Some Jazz," and "Take Me to the Land of Jazz."

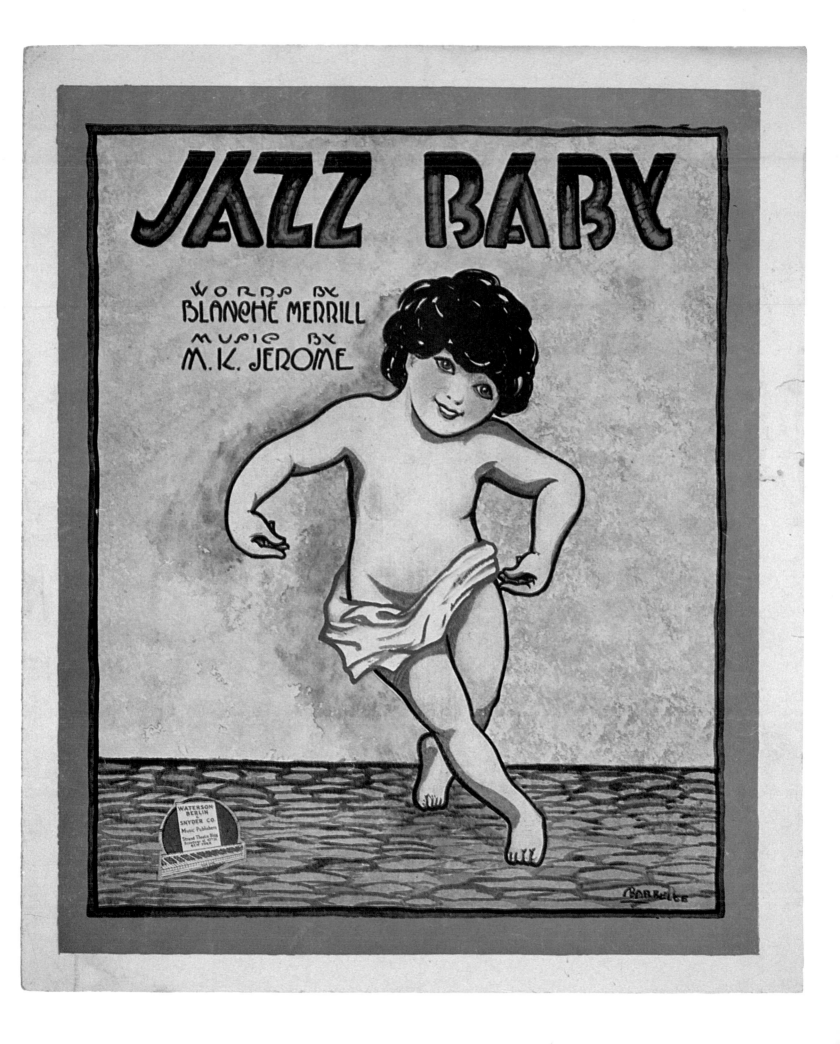

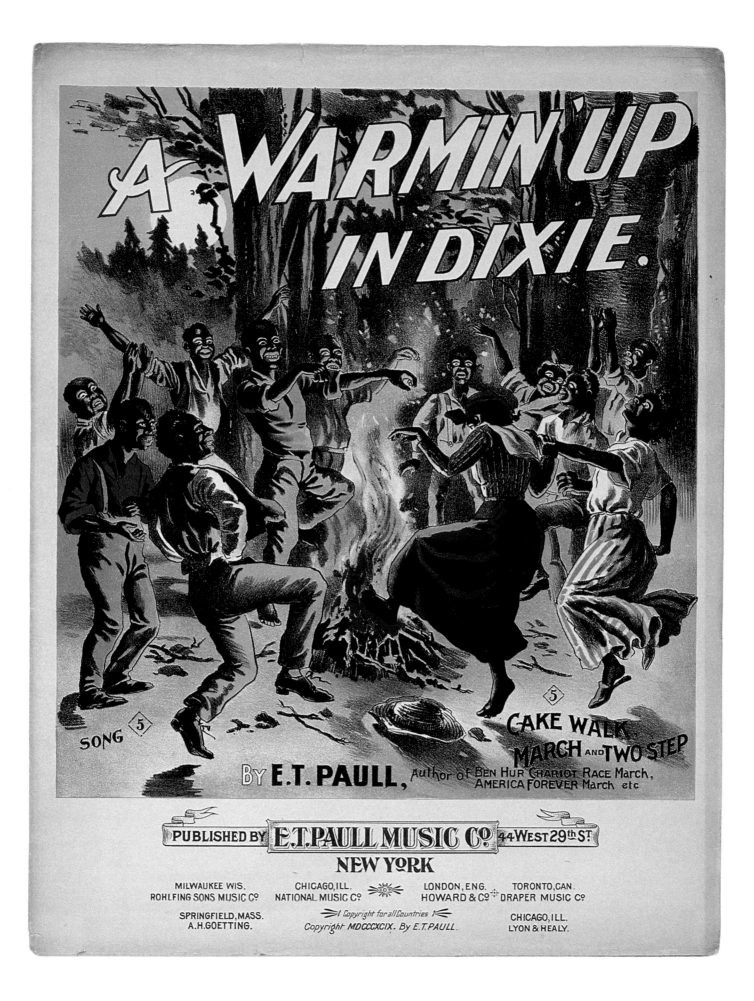

"DARKTOWN IS OUT TONIGHT"

By the beginning of the twentieth century, black popular song was at a major crossroad. Traditional spirituals were no longer as fashionable as they had been in the 1870s and 1880s. Three new kinds of black secular music—ragtime, blues, and jazz—were emerging as the era's most promising popular genres. Black minstrelsy was peaking as an entertainment form, setting the stage for the decline of the coon song.

The first black production to openly break with the entrenched blackface minstrel tradition was "The Creole Show," organized in New York City in 1890. The show was bankrolled and produced by Sam Jack, a local white vaudeville theater owner. He hired some of the best-known black minstrel performers of the era, including Sam Lucas, Billy Jackson, Fred Piper, Irving Jones, and Bob Cole. Deviating from minstrel convention, the show also featured a female chorus line and a female mistress of ceremonies who introduced the acts and skits. After auditions and rehearsals, "The Creole Show" went out on the road, performing in Boston and then in Chicago during the 1893 Columbus World Exposition. On returning to New York, it enjoyed a short run at an off-Broadway theater before closing.

Its popularity with predominantly white audiences made a strong impression on John Isham, who worked as a booking agent for the show. In 1895, he financed a similar black variety show called "The Octoroons." It featured the popular minstrel song-and-dance team of Walter Smart and George Williams performing their curious trademark song "No Coon Too Black for Me." Also with the show were Bob Cole and his future wife, Stella Wiley, a talented comedienne and singer who would play an important role in Cole's career as a successful theatrical songwriter and producer.

Isham next produced a more upscale show called "Oriental America." Its grand finale featured classically trained black vocalists William Elkins, Sidney Woodward, and Maggie Scott singing a medley of songs from famous operas. The show, which had a short run at the Palmer Theater on Broadway in 1896, was the first black musical revue to play for a white audience on show business' most revered street of dreams.

The same year that "Oriental America" included opera standards in its stage production, another black show tried a similar approach. Black Patti's Troubadours was organized in 1896 by the white managers of Sissieretta Jones, a highly acclaimed African American opera singer who had just returned to the United States from a triumphant European tour. "Black Patti" was a sobriquet given to Jones by the European press which compared her to Adelina Patti, the reigning diva of Italian opera. Hoping to capitalize on her European publicity, the managers put together a stage extravaganza which showcased "Black Patti" in an "operatic Kaleidoscope." To fill out the show, Jones' managers hired Bob Cole. Along with his new wife and Billy Johnson, a talented minstrel veteran, Cole

Highly sought after by sheet music collectors, vivid covers like this one were E. T. Paull's trademark. Other songs Paull released were "The Midnight Fire Alarm" and "The Chariot Race of Ben Hur." Much of African American life was unknown to white audiences; this cover seems to be addressing their desire to fill in the gaps in their knowledge with fantasy and mystery.

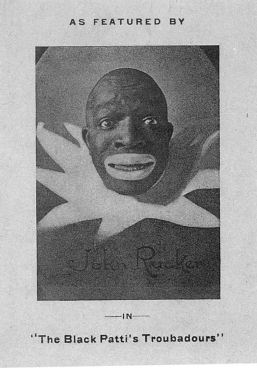

AS FEATURED BY

John Rucker

—IN—

"The Black Patti's Troubadours"

John Rucker sang Bert William's trademark song, "Nobody," in a 1905 production by Black Patti's Troubadours.

scripted a short "musical farce" to follow the operatic segment.

The farce featured Bob Cole as Willie Wayside, a genial tramp, and Billy Johnson portraying Jim Flimflammer, a slippery con artist. The most popular song in the skit initially called "At Jolly Coon-ey Island" was Cole's "The Blow That Killed My Father." Unfortunately, he lost his rights to all compositions used in the farce in a legal dispute with the managers of Black Patti's Troubadours. However, the outline of the story and the characters from "At Jolly Coon-ey Island" later reappeared in Cole's first full-length musical production, *A Trip to Coontown*.

Bob Cole's bitter lesson at the hands of

"Black Patti's" managers gave him the incentive to establish his own production company for his next stage venture. He teamed up with Billy Johnson again, and they expanded their Willie Wayside and Jim Flimflammer routine into *A Trip to Coontown* in 1898. The storyline to the musical farce remained weak, however, and the new music for it was uninspiring. The show relied on cameo appearances by Javin Roan, "The Cuban Nightingale," and Lloyd G. Gibbs, "The Greatest Living Black Tenor." After a brief run off-Broadway and a short tour, *A Trip to Coontown* closed.

The next phase of Bob Cole's stage career proved to be his most productive, thanks to his new association with Rosamond and James Weldon Johnson. The trio collaborated in writing a series of successful Broadway show tunes in the early 1900s, in particular, "Under the Bamboo Tree," "Congo Love Song," and "My Castle on the Nile." During this same period, Cole and Rosamond Johnson developed a classy act to showcase their songs. In 1906, they wrote and produced their first black musical together, the critically acclaimed *Shoo-fly Regiment*.

The musical's stage drama featured Bob Cole as Hunter Wilson, a black college graduate living in Alabama who forsakes his promising career as a teacher to volunteer for duty in the Spanish-American War. Black starlet Fannie Wise played his sweetheart, Rosa Maxwell, who disapproves of war and breaks off their engagement when he joins the U.S. Army. Hunter goes off to the war with the other

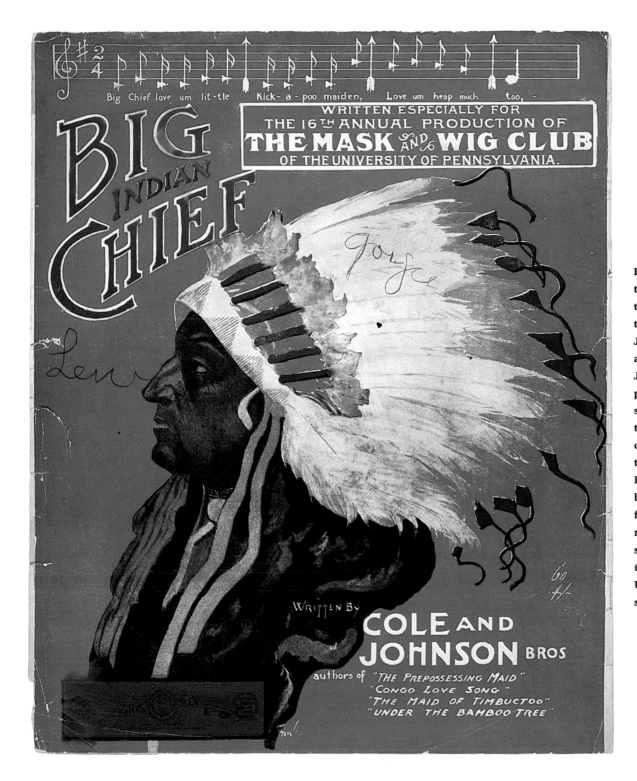

Between the turn of the century and 1908, the African American team of Bob Cole, J. Rosamond Johnson, and James Weldon Johnson was the most prolific of all popular songwriters, with more than 200 songs to their credit. Many of their tunes were written for Broadway productions, but they also composed for the popular music market. This particular song was written for a theatrical club at the University of Pennsylvania.

Fanny Brice rose to stardom with this song in the 1910 Ziegfeld Follies. It was written by veteran black composers Will Marion Cook and Joe Jordan. Other African American entertainers represented in this Follies included Will Vodery, who led the orchestra in the Follies Roof Garden series. Future Follies featured more black-written songs, among them "At the Ball" and "The Darktown Poker Club."

black enlistees and eventually returns a hero. He and Rose are reunited and get married in the final scene.

Although something of a soap opera, the stage show was admirable for the positive—even patriotic—roles given to its black male characters. Also, it portrayed the story's romance between the two leading African American characters in a thoughtful and dignified manner, perhaps a first for the Broadway stage. In retrospect, *The Shoo-fly Regiment* was a landmark in the transformation of the black stage image from comic buffoonery to serious artistry.

Bob Cole and the Johnson Brothers collaborated on one final musical together, *Red Moon,* in 1908. Advertised as "a sensation in red and black," it was their most ambitious theater project. The show attempted to highlight the musical cultures of both Native Americans and African Americans and included songs based on the folk music of both groups. The storyline featured Cole and Johnson as suitors of a beautiful maiden named Minnehaha, played by Abbie Mitchell, whose father is Indian and whose mother is black. Much of the action takes place out West in Indian territory. Cole and Johnson had actually visited an Apache reservation in their earlier travels, and among the material used in *Red Moon* was some they had collected while there.

The musical was well received on Broadway and embarked on a national tour. But Bob Cole suffered a nervous breakdown, and the remaining shows had to be canceled. After a lengthy illness, he committed suicide in 1911. Cole would be sorely missed in black theatrical circles. A key figure in bringing black musicals to the Broadway stage, he was also in the forefront of the struggle to undermine the old blackface minstrel stereotypes by creating more humane and positive black stage images.

Another black composer who rivaled Bob Cole as a major innovator in black musical theater during this period was Will Marion Cook. The same year that Cole produced *A Trip to Coontown* (1898), Cook produced his first full-length musical comedy, *Clorindy, or The Origin of the Cakewalk.* The stage show was inspired by and written for the comedy team of Bert Williams and George Walker, who had popularized the cakewalk on the New York stage in the mid-1890s. But at the last minute, Williams and Walker were unable to appear in *Clorindy*; instead, Ernest Hogan was hired as the star attraction.

The music for the show was composed by Cook; the lyrics were written by his friend, Paul Lawrence Dunbar. The famous African American poet was renowned for his command of the black vernacular; his talents were evident in songs like "Who Dat Say Chicken in Dis Crowd":

> *Who dat say chicken in dis crowd?*
> *Speak de word a-gin and speak it loud.*
> *Blame de lan' let the white folks rule it*
> *I'se a lookin' fu' a pullet*
> *Who dat say chicken in dis crowd?*

Clorindy, or The Origin of the Cakewalk catapulted Cook into the limelight of New York show business. The next year, he produced his second full-length musical, *Jes Lak White Folks*, but it was not as well received by the critics and public as his first effort. For a while, his career floundered. Then after the turn of the century, Will Cook joined forces with his favorite performers, Bert Williams and George Walker. Together they wrote and produced the popular duo's first Broadway musical, *In Dahomey.*

Significantly, the setting for much of this stage comedy was the West African country of Dahomey. The choice of this site was a conscious ploy to get away from blackface stereotypes. In their place, the writers created dignified African characters and sly novelty songs promoting the "back to Africa" theme:

> *Evah dahkey is a king*
> *Royalty is jes' de ting*
> *Ef yo' social life is a bungle*
> *Jes' go back to yo' jungle*
> *An' remember dat you daddy was a king.*

The trio collaborated on two more musical comedies before the end of the decade: *In Abyssinia* (1906) and *Bandana Land* (1908). In the former, the setting is once again Africa; likewise, the African characters are again depicted as members of a noble and humane race. Ironically and in spite of themselves, the leading African American characters, played by Williams and Walker, still tended to fall back on the comic buffoon stereotypes from minstrelsy. *Bandana Land* took place in the United States; it had a much stronger plot, and the characters were more believable than their predecessors. With this Broadway musical, the comedy team of Williams and Walker achieved their greatest success. Unfortunately, George Walker became ill while the show was on tour, and he died of syphilis a few years later.

The first wave of black musical comedies peaked with the production of *Bandana Land* and *Red Moon*. By 1910, they had vanished from the Broadway stage and would not make a comeback there until after the First World War. One primary reason for this decline was the deaths of George Walker, Bob Cole, and Ernest Hogan. Another was the formation in New York City and Chicago of black theatrical troupes which initially shunned traditional white theater audiences in favor of black ones.

In Chicago, the first major black theater group was organized by Billy King. The Pekin Stock Company, as it was called, was based at the Pekin Theater. The best-known entertainers to get their start with the company were Flournoy Miller and Aubrey Lyles, the soon-to-be famous comedy song-and-dance team.

In New York, the Lincoln and Lafayette theaters in Harlem became the center of a new "black Broadway." The Lafayette Theater sponsored the city's premier black theater troupe, the

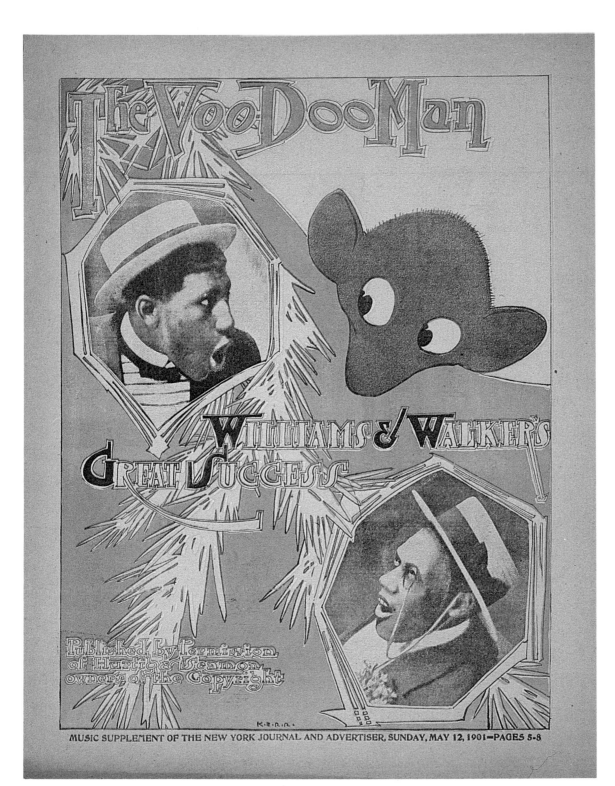

Widespread throughout the South and especially in New Orleans, voodoo was brought to the New York stage by Williams and Walker. The imagery of spells, charms, and curses of this African-based religious cult worked its way into both twentieth-century jazz and popular music. In their shows, George Walker always dressed as the dandy, Bert Williams as the bumpkin. This particular piece of sheet music was originally a newspaper supplement.

At the turn of the century, Bert Williams was one-half of a successful stage team known as Williams and Walker. After George Walker fell ill with the syphilis that was to kill him, Williams joined the Ziegfeld Follies as a solo act. A dignified man who had studied pantomime in France and understood all elements of comedy, he made as much money in his prime as the president of the United States.

Lafayette Players. They staged some of the era's most innovative black musicals, as well as serious dramas. In the process, they also trained a new generation of performers and actors, including Abbie Mitchell, Laura Bowman, Edna Thomas, Charles Gilpin, Charles Moore, "Babe" Townsend, and Clarence Muse.

The emergence of ragtime, blues, and jazz coincided with three new developments in the commercial music industry which would also have a far-reaching impact on the evolution and scope of black popular song and popular song in general. They were the invention of the phonograph, the rise of Tin Pan Alley, and the organization of a black vaudeville theater circuit.

The mechanical phonograph was the brainchild of Thomas Edison, invented in 1877. As early as the 1890s, a small consumer market had begun to develop for phonograph machines and the crude cylinder recordings that were played on them. The most fashionable of these were opera titles, sentimental ballads, marches, ragtime numbers, and coon songs.

Only a handful of African American entertainers were given the opportunity to record on cylinder. The first was George W. Johnson, who cut his minstrel signature piece, "The Whistling Coon," for Edison's company shortly after it opened for business. Another black performer captured on cylinder recordings was Blind Boone, who made a series of records based on his ragtime composi-

tions after the turn of the century. By that time, the cylinder recording was being eclipsed by the disc recording, which improved the sound fidelity somewhat and was easier to handle.

During the first two decades of disc recordings, the major record companies all but ignored African American talent. The Columbia Record Company, established in 1899, excluded black entertainers from their recording studios until the 1920s. Bert Williams auditioned for Columbia, and when he was turned down, the famous black comedian approached Columbia's chief rival, the Victor Talking Machine Company, founded in 1901. Sensing that Williams might be as popular with both black and white record buyers as he was with black and white vaudeville patrons, the new Victor label was shrewd enough to record him. Between 1902 and 1904, Williams cut 15 records for them, most of which were either novelty tunes or comedy routines from his stage repertoire. Bert Williams' best-selling disc from this period, "Elder Eatmore's Sermon," was a comic monologue that was the centerpiece of his act; it sold more than 500,000 copies.

The surprising commercial success of "Elder Eatmore's Sermon" encouraged the Victor Talking Machine Company to adopt a more liberal policy on recording African American talent. In the wake of Bert Williams' hit, Victor released six records by the Dinwiddie Colored Quartet, including familiar novelty songs from minstrelsy as well as traditional spirituals like "Steal Away" and "My

Way Is Cloudy." In response to Victor's success with black musical releases, in particular the spirituals, Columbia broke its self-imposed color line and signed the Fisk Jubilee Singers for a series of recordings just prior to World War I.

The decade's biggest commercial breakthrough for black recording artists came in 1914, when James Reese Europe's Society Orchestra recorded some dance numbers for Victor as part of a series sponsored by Vernon and Irene Castle, a popular white dance team. Europe's Society Orchestra was made up of members of the Clef Club, a black musicians benevolent society he had helped to organize in New York in 1910. At the center of the club's musical activities was a core group of talented composers and arrangers, including William Tyers, Will Marion Cook, Will Vodery, Tim Brymn, and Ford Dabney.

Up until the end of World War I, only the exceptional African American vocalist, choral group, or orchestra was given the opportunity to record. During this same period, however, the two major record companies did release a wide variety of black material covered by white entertainers, and this trend would continue to be influential in the years ahead. Columbia Record's catalogue listed a "Negro Novelty" section, while the Victor label advertised "Up-to-date comic songs in Negro dialect." Both companies also referred to their black-inspired releases as "coon songs," "Ethiopian airs," and "plantation airs."

Al Jolson, May Irwin, and Sophie Tucker, all major recording stars, were among the early white performers who covered black songs. Al Jolson recorded a number of the minstrel songs he performed in blackface on the New York stage. May Irwin was one of the first white vocalists to popularize coon songs in the 1890s, and after the turn of the century, she recorded a series of these, including "Mammie Come Kiss Your Honey" and "The Bully Song." "The Bully Song" was adapted from a black urban folksong by Charles Trevathan, a white tunesmith who incorporated an array of blackface minstrel stereotypes into his version. The first verse went as follows:

I was standin' down the Mobile Buck just to cut a shine
Some coon across my smeller swiped a water melon rin'
I drowned my steel dat gemmen to fin'
I riz up like a black cloud and took a look aroun'
There was dat new bully standin' on the ground
I've been lookin' for you nigger and I got you found.

The most successful of the early white entertainers who specialized in performing and recording black popular songs was Sophie Tucker. A Russian-born immigrant, she broke into show business in New York City just after 1900. Because she was a robust, heavy-set woman, she did not

"YOU'RE IN THE RIGHT CHURCH BUT THE WRONG PEW"

FEATURED BY BERT A. WILLIAMS IN "BANDANA LAND"

The GREATEST OF WILLIAMS AND WALKERS GREAT BIG HITS

By Cecil Mack (R. C. McPHERSON) and Chris Smith

WRITERS OF HE'S A COUSIN OF MINE ALL IN DOWN AND OUT

THE GOTHAM-ATTUCKS MUSIC COMPANY. THE HOUSE OF MELODY NEW YORK

The first African American-owned music publishing firm in New York was the Gotham-Attucks Music Publishing Company. In its six years of existence, "The House of Melody" published music by many black songsters. The covers broke new ground because they did not resort to the racial stereotyping typical of other companies, and although Gotham-Attucks did include some coon songs in its catalog, they were never labeled as such.

Some white composers frequented black bars and clubrooms with the sole purpose of stealing songs, then publishing them under their own names. One group specializing in this maneuver was known as the "cuff boys." Many black songsters, Irving Jones and Chris Smith among them, were musically illiterate. According to one publisher, Jones probably lost as many tunes as he wrote.

measure up to the beauty standards set by the local producers of the vaudeville shows. Consequently, they forced her to wear blackface and perform coon songs, likening her to the antebellum "Mammy" stereotype, until she was able to prove that she could attract an audience without them. However, when Tucker did away with the blackface and the coon songs, she continued to perform and record African American music and scored the biggest hits of her career with ragtime and blues releases written by black composers. They included Shelton Brooks' "Some of These Days" and "The Darktown Strutters Ball," as well as W. C. Handy's classic "St. Louis Blues."

The rise of Tin Pan Alley gave the commercial music industry almost total control over the structure, scope, and direction of popular song in the United States. In the late 1800s, the sale of sheet music for home entertainment was the major source of income for composers and the music publishing firms that handled their songs. Many of the larger and more powerful firms were located in New York City along 28th Street, between Broadway and Fifth Avenue. By the turn of the century, this corridor was commonly referred to as Tin Pan Alley. Here the music publishing firms hired legions of professional tunesmiths to come up with the songs they sold back to the public as sheet music. After 1900, the firms began selling their wares to the record companies as well. Tin Pan Alley songwriting was organized on an assembly-line basis; songs were mass-produced according to the prevailing song formulas. Moreover, the music publishing business was quick to expropriate any and all new black musical genres, providing they proved to be profitable. In the process of transforming ragtime and blues into commercial products, Tin Pan Alley standardized the music, diluted its more complex rhythms, and trivialized its lyrical content.

Tin Pan Alley received a windfall in 1909, when the first copyright law was passed by the United States Congress. The law stipulated that copyright owners had exclusive rights to perform and reproduce their work. It also gave the publishing firm filing for the copyright 50 percent of ownership and royalty rights. This meant that the new record companies had to pay royalties to the composers of the music and/or to the publishing firms that owned at least half of the copyright in question.

Five years after the new law went into effect, the American Society of Composers, Authors, and Publishers (ASCAP) was founded in New York City. This new trade organization was established to monitor the commercial performances of its client members' compositions, collect royalty fees from the record labels and other music users, and distribute that income to the appropriate composers, lyricists, and publishers. From its inception, ASCAP was an elite Tin Pan Alley operation catering to the most successful music publishing firms and songwriters in the city. Very few outsiders were permitted to join the organization; this was especially true for African Americans trying to find a niche in the burgeoning music industry.

The songwriter, Kerry Mills, and the publisher, F. A. Mills, were the same person. Mills, a white man who was head of the University of Michigan School of Music's violin department, wrote this number as a protest against coon songs, which he felt maligned African Americans. With the introduction of cakewalks, cover art changed. The cover for this song, with its detailed scene depicting cartoonish blacks, served as the basic style, copied by virtually all publishers of the genre.

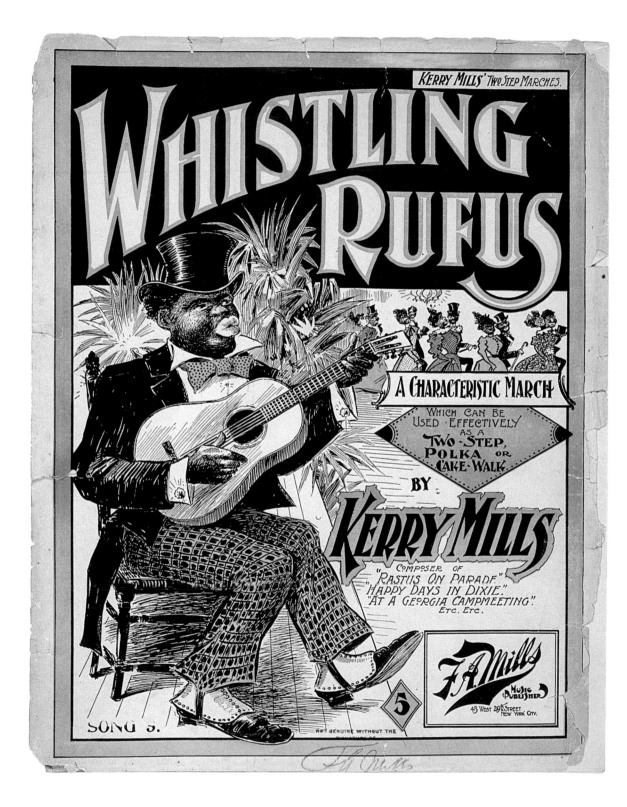

The similarities between this cover and "At a Georgia Campmeeting" are characteristic of sheet music written and published by the same person. Although "Whistling Rufus" was normally performed as a cakewalk, Mills wanted to reassure the purchaser that it was quite acceptable to dance a two-step or a polka to the tune. The dandy portrayed here was a familiar image, used on the stage with great success by George Walker.

This song is another pseudonegro piece meant to push all the right buttons— "ragtime," "cakewalk"— and play on white audiences' fascination with what they saw as black culture without causing offense: the dusky-faced couple on the cover even appear to have white features.

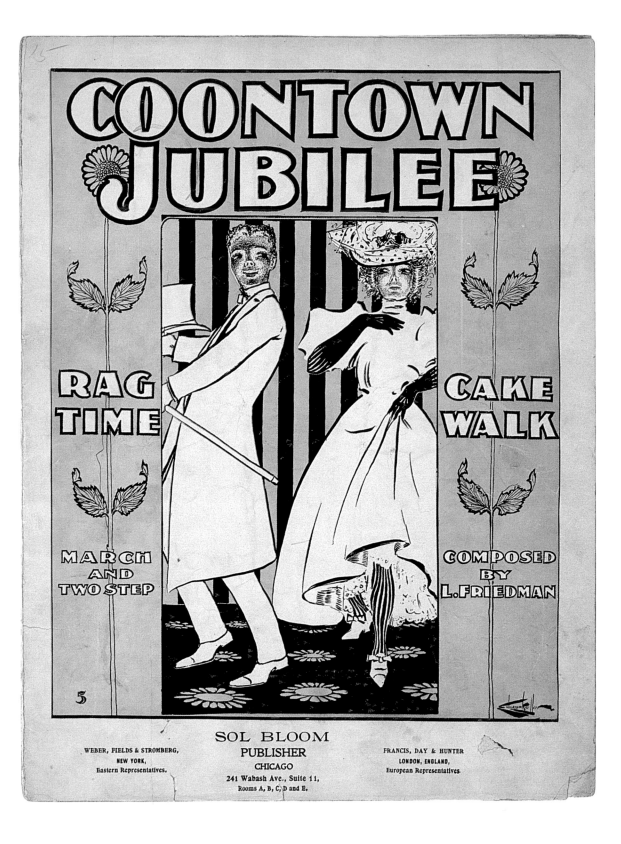

The advent of black musical theater had been a milestone in the transition from black minstrelsy to black vaudeville. The distance between these two cultural institutions was in many ways remarkable. For example, up until the twentieth century, black minstrelsy was an all-male club. Black vaudeville, on the other hand, always included African American women as supporting cast members and in some cases even headliners. Another major difference was evident in the stage settings. Plantation scenery and costumes dominated the black minstrel shows, whereas the black vaudeville shows thrived on multiple settings from urban America to mother Africa.

In the comedy routines and characters, the entrenched blackface stereotypes recycled in black minstrelsy were challenged by new modes of comic discourse. More doubled-voiced humor, parody, and signifying, the African American art of verbal warfare, came to the forefront. In addition, a much wider range of black images and storytellers was presented on stage, and black entertainers had much more leeway to develop their own characters and routines. Last but not least, the popular music changed profoundly. The sentimental ballads and coon songs from the golden age of minstrelsy gave way to ragtime tunes and the blues. This new music was much more danceable, its rhythms more fluid and multilayered.

Only the economic order remained relatively unchanged during these unprecedented cultural shifts. There were a few notable exceptions to this rule, especially during the rise of black vaudeville, but in general, white entrepreneurs controlled the financial aspects of black show business.

The growth of a black vaudeville theater circuit based in the major urban centers of the United States began even before the turn of the century. As early as the 1890s, theaters which catered almost exclusively to black entertainers were springing up throughout the country. During this period, the more prosperous minstrel troupes began appearing before white, and in some cases, black audiences in the new urban theaters, most of which were owned and operated by white businessmen.

These show business entrepreneurs were notorious for the poor wages they paid black entertainers, and for their unwillingness to provide clean and adequate facilities for the performers. In spite of this, their theaters became the arenas for a black vaudeville circuit that flourished over the next three decades.

In 1907, a white Memphis theater owner, F. A. Barrasso, attempted to organize the first chain of southern theaters to feature black entertainment into a vaudeville network. By formalizing the procedures for booking black minstrel troupes into these theaters, Barrasso hoped to make them more efficient and thus more profitable for the owners, if not the entertainers. Two years later his brother, Anselmo Barrasso, took over the venture and founded the Theater Owners Booking Association (TOBA). He built up a string of member theaters

When her husband George Walker became ill, Ada Overton Walker dressed as his character and took his place on stage, earning rave reviews.

not only in the South, but also in the Midwest and along the Eastern Seaboard.

On the eve of World War I, the TOBA vaudeville circuit was the major source of employment for black entertainers. To its credit, the TOBA provided valuable experience and exposure for innumerable black performers and musicians who might not have had an opportunity to break into show business otherwise. In addition, it proved to be a steppingstone for a handful of the more popular black entertainers who were also offered employment at the major white vaudeville theaters of the day, where the salaries were much more substantial. Most black performers, however, remained locked into the TOBA, where the wages, facilities, and working conditions inspired the well-known employee definition of the organization: "TOBA—Tough On Black Asses!"

Nevertheless, the TOBA gave many black entertainers their only real opportunity to perform, sometimes even before discerning black audiences. Moreover, the theater network offered the allure of fame and fortune to its employees. Like the black minstrel shows it eclipsed, black vaudeville was one of the few means by which African Americans could acquire wealth and social status. Overflow crowds packed the TOBA shows and lavished both praise and scorn on the featured entertainers. In a short time, the shows became a major cultural activity in the new black urban enclaves, and their star performers became cultural heroes and heroines. Understandably, aspiring black entertainers flocked to the TOBA circuit.

The variety shows and revues first staged at the TOBA theaters by black entertainers were invariably organized around a few star attractions. The personnel involved in these shows included the musicians who played in the band and a female chorus line of dancers. The acts that received top billing were diverse: comedy teams, song-and-dance artists, solo instrumentalists, and novelty acts.

A number of husband-and-wife teams were active on the black vaudeville circuit. The best known were Butterbeans and Susie, Coot Grant and Kid Sock Wilson, and George Williams and Bessie Smith (no relation to the famous blues singer). Butterbeans and Susie were in real life Jody and Susie Edwards; they sang duets together and developed a satirical comedy routine based on their marital squabbles. Leola and Wesley Wilson, known on stage as Coot Grant and Kid Sock Wilson, were seasoned vaudeville performers and songwriters. During their long career, they co-authored more than 400 songs, the most famous of which, "Gimme a Pigfoot," eventually became one of blues queen Bessie Smith's trademark numbers. George and Bessie Williams (she used Smith as her stage name) were both talented vocalists. He also played the piano and wrote his own songs, and together they made a series of recordings for the Columbia label after World War I.

The leading male entertainers with the TOBA prior to the First World War included Hamtree Harrington, Dusty Fletcher, Sammy Lewis, Billy King, and Tom Fletcher. They were joined by a new contingent of female stars like the Whiteman Sisters, Ethel Waters a.k.a. Sweet Mama Stringbean, Fannie Wise, Ada Myers, Ella Moore, Ma Rainey, and Bessie Smith.

Ma Rainey, the legendary "Mother of the Blues," was born Gertrude Pridgett in Columbus, Georgia, in 1886. She was drawn to minstrelsy as a teenager and appeared in a local musical revue called "A Bunch of Blackberries" at the age of 14. Four years later, she married William "Pa" Rainey, a seasoned black entertainer on tour with the Rabbit Foot Minstrels. Soon thereafter, the couple embarked on a 12-year career as a minstrel song-and-dance team, during which Gertrude acquired the stage name "Ma" even though she was still a young woman.

Ma and Pa Rainey built up a large following in the South, performing with many of the top minstrel troupes of the day. They toured during the summer and fall, then spent the winter in New Orleans. There Ma Rainey worked with many of the city's most accomplished jazz musicians, including King Oliver, Kid Ory, Sidney Bechet, Pops Foster, and a youthful Louis Armstrong.

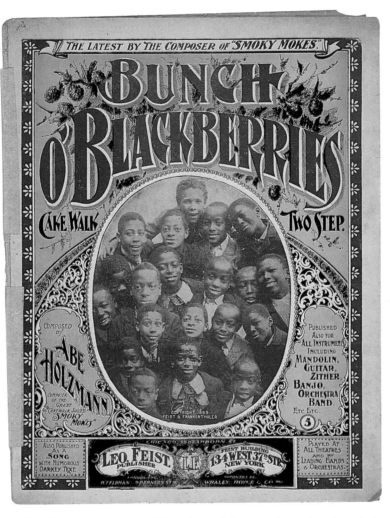

This sheet and the one on the following page show how so-called black music was marketed. The similarities are intentional. "Bunch O' Blackberries," "Smoky Mokes," and the third in the series, "Hunky Dory," were actually composed by a German-born white man, Abe Holzmann, known for his classical compositions. All three cakewalks were made famous after being performed by bandmaster John Philip Sousa.

Ma Rainey claimed to have first heard the blues while on tour in 1902 in a small Missouri town. There a young woman approached her with a song about a no-good man who had left her with a broken heart. Ma was so impressed with this "strange and poignant song" that she immediately incorporated it into her stage act. More than likely, this fateful encounter actually took place in 1904 during her initial tour with Pa Rainey. In any event, by 1905, Ma Rainey's blues were the highlight of

"Smoky Mokes" was a popular instrumental cakewalk. The title can be traced to various blackface teams active in vaudeville ("moke" was a slang term for a black person). One performer who called himself Smoky Moke was a particular favorite of turn-of-the-century New York City society. Moke's partner was Captain Bojangles, who later dropped "Captain" and became known as Bill "Bojangles" Robinson.

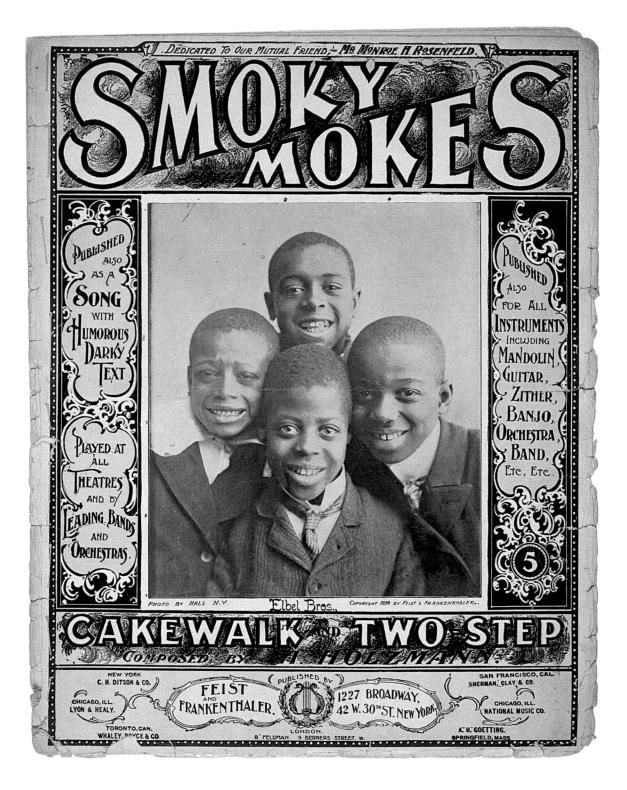

her stage act; they were attracting the attention not only of new fans, but also of the local press in towns where she performed. Almost overnight, she became the first black female minstrel star to be identified with the blues.

Ma and Pa Rainey's last performances as a duo took place in the mid-1910s, when they worked as headliners for Tolliver's Circus and Minstrel Extravaganza, billed as "Rainey & Rainey: Assassinators of the Blues." After two years with Tolliver's troupe, the team went their separate ways. By that time, Ma Rainey had earned the sobriquet, "Mother of the Blues," and was a well-established star in her own right. In 1917, she organized her own touring company, billed as "Madam Gertrude Rainey and the Georgia Smart Set." The show featured a female chorus line and a small string band, which backed up when Rainey was singing on stage.

A number of people who witnessed Ma Rainey's stage act commented on her uncanny ability to strike a responsive chord in her audiences. Black poet and scholar Sterling A. Brown, who wrote a famous poem paying tribute to her talents, recalled, "She wouldn't have to sing the words, she would just moan and the audience would moan along with her….She was a person of the folk, very simple and direct. Her music went straight to the heart."

Ma Rainey had an early influence on Bessie Smith, the female vocalist destined to be the most popular black performer and recording artist of the post-World War I era. Smith broke into show business in her hometown of Chattanooga, Tennessee, at the age of 18. Her older brother Clarence had earlier joined Moses Stoke's minstrel troupe as a comedian. Upon returning to Chattanooga with the show in 1912, he arranged for his sister to audition for it, and she was hired on as a dancer.

Moses Stoke's star attraction at the time was the team of Ma and Pa Rainey. Out on tour together, Ma Rainey and Bessie Smith struck up a close friendship that lasted for the rest of their lives. Smith, no doubt influenced by the older woman, would later record two of Ma Rainey's trademark blues, "Boll Weevil Blues" and "Moonshine Blues." But less than a year after joining the show, Bessie Smith moved on to Atlanta, Georgia, where she was employed at one of the TOBA's most prestigious showcases, Charles Bailey's 81 Theater. Her starting salary was only $10 a week, but her dramatic singing style brought in a lot extra in tips.

The song she was most closely associated with during her years in Atlanta is "Weary Blues," a common folk blues first published by a St. Louis ragtime pianist named Artie Matthews in 1915. People who saw Bessie Smith perform during this period remembered her as a raw and awkward entertainer. Yet they also acknowledged that she was already an inspired blues singer with the ability to dominate a show; audiences were spellbound by her vocal pyrotechnics. In the next few years, her career as a blues queen would skyrocket.

BOB COLE AND THE JOHNSON BROTHERS

Bob Cole was born in Athens, Georgia, on July 1, 1868. He began his songwriting career in 1893 with the publication of "Parthenia Takes a Likin' to a Coon" and "In Shin Bone Alley." His earliest theatrical experiences included work with both Sam T. Jack's "The Creole Show," the first African American show to break from the strict minstrel tradition of all male performers, and the All Star Stock Company at Worth's Museum in New York, the first such company organized by African Americans.

When he was 27 years old and performing with Black Patti's Troubadours, Cole was engaged by the Troubadours' producers to write an entire show with Billy Johnson, his first collaborator. After a dispute over ownership of his music, Cole and Johnson left to organize Cole's own company. Elaborating on his early short sketches, he created a full-length musical which was performed off-Broadway in New York's Third Avenue Theater during the 1898-99 season. *A Trip To Coontown* was the first musical entirely written, performed, produced, and owned by African Americans. Unlike other black entertainments of the time, Cole's production had a book and lyrics that could sustain a dramatic subplot. After the show closed, Cole and Billy Johnson broke off their working relationship, and Cole met the two men with whom he was to create his most successful songs.

J. Rosamond and James Weldon Johnson were born in Jacksonville, Florida, James Weldon in 1871 and Rosamond in 1873. By the age of four, Rosamond was already an accomplished pianist. Later he studied classical music at the New England Conservatory of Music in Boston, but left after six years because his real interest lay in musical comedy. By age 23, he was touring as a vocalist with the company of "Oriental America."

His brother James Weldon studied both piano and guitar. After graduating from Atlanta University, he took charge of the Stanton Public School, wrote poetry, and founded a short-lived newspaper called *The Daily American*. Later he studied law and became the first African American in Florida to seek and gain admission to the bar through open examination.

Around 1898, Rosamond returned to Jacksonville, and at his insistence, the brothers began work on their first musical, *Toloso*, which James Weldon described in *Along This Way* as "a comic opera satirizing the new American imperialism" after the Spanish-American War. In 1899, they decided to go to New York to seek their fortunes.

Though *Toloso* was never produced, its songs were later used in Broadway musicals, and it introduced the Johnsons to others in the business, including Oscar Hammerstein, Williams and Walker, and Will Marion Cook. It also introduced them to their future partner, Bob Cole.

Bob Cole, James Weldon Johnson, and J. Rosamond Johnson.

From the very beginning of their relationship, Bob Cole and the Johnson brothers seemed focused on one major goal: elevating the lyrical sophistication of Black songs. The team's first collaboration was "Louisiana Lize," a love song written in a new lyrical style which left out the watermelons, razors, and hot mamas typical of coon songs. For $50, they sold the singing rights to May Irwin, who was then known as a singer of coon songs. Irwin used it in her next show, *The Belle of Bridgeport*, and the song was later published by Jos. P. Stern and Co. Its success encouraged the team that their goal was not out

of reach, and during the next seven years, Cole, Johnson, and Johnson wrote more than 200 songs, working in a unique form of collaboration in which they each took turns writing words, composing melody, and acting as critic.

By 1901, Bob Cole and Rosamond Johnson had put together a sophisticated vaudeville act. Dressed in evening clothes, Rosamond played classical works on the piano, then the pair sang their own compositions and ended the act with a soft-shoe routine by Cole. According to Rosamond, they were walking back uptown after a performance one day when

59

he began to hum the African American spiritual "Nobody Knows the Trouble I've Seen." Hearing the song, Cole got the idea to rearrange it and work it into their act. When Rosamond objected that this was sacrilegious, Cole responded, "What kind of a musician are you anyway? Been to the Boston Conservatory and can't change a little old tune around." By the time Rosamond finally conceded, Cole had already written the words in an invented dialect.

If you lak-a me
lak I lak-a you,
an we lak-a both the same,
I lak-a say,
this very day,
I lak-a change your name.

The resulting song, "Under the Bamboo Tree," sold more than 400,000 copies, making it one of the biggest sellers of its day.

With Cole's and Rosamond Johnson's popular vaudeville act touring much of the time, James Weldon Johnson began to pursue other interests. At the request of Charles Anderson, a leading black New York politician, he managed

the Colored Republican's Club. He also attended Columbia University, studied English, and began work on a novel, *The Auto-Biography of an Ex-Colored Man*, which was published in 1912.

In 1903, the trio signed a three-year contract with Klaw and Erlanger, major Broadway producers. In exchange for a monthly salary and royalties, they agreed to write exclusively for Klaw and Erlanger's shows.

When the contract expired, having earned them more than $25,000 a year in royalties, Bob Cole and Rosamond Johnson decided to resume their vaudeville routine. With James Weldon as their manager, they toured throughout the United States and performed in Paris and London. Legend has it that "Under the Bamboo Tree" was the last thing they heard as they set sail from New York for Europe and the first thing they heard when they arrived in Paris.

Following their successful tour, Cole and Rosamond Johnson started their own theatrical company. In 1906, they produced and starred in a musical called *The Shoo-Fly Regiment*. After helping to write the songs for this show, James Weldon decided that it would be the last piece of work they would do together.

Charles Anderson, now a member of the Roosevelt Administration, encouraged him to join the foreign service, and soon after, James Weldon Johnson went to Venezuela as the United States consul. In 1909, he was appointed consul to Nicaragua where he served for over three years.

In 1908, Bob Cole and Rosamond Johnson produced and starred in a new show with an Indian theme. *Red Moon* was called the best African American show that had ever been produced because of its superior book and well-written songs.

Soon after *Red Moon* closed, Cole's health began to fail. Although he recovered briefly and toured with Rosamond for a time in a new vaudeville act, he fell ill again. Rumors of syphilis began to surface. Cole died on August 2, 1911.

Rosamond Johnson went on to write the music and conduct the orchestra for the 1911 revue "Hello Paris." It was the first time an African American conducted a white orchestra for a performance with a white cast in a New York theater. In 1912, Oscar Hammerstein appointed Rosamond musical director of his Grand Opera House in London. On June third of the following year, Rosamond married Nora Floyd, and after two years in London, they returned to New York and started the Music School Settlement for Colored People.

In 1917, Rosamond directed a singing orchestra which appeared in a series of ground-breaking plays given by The Coloured Players at the Garden Theater in Madison Square Garden. The plays opened on April 5. The United States declared war on Germany the following day, and although the production continued for a while, the war finally brought it to a close.

Rosamond joined the army and served as a second lieutenant with the 15th Regiment. He appeared in *Porgy and Bess* in 1935, but never wrote another musical comedy. Rosamond Johnson died on November 11, 1954.

James Weldon Johnson continued to engage in a variety of activities. For ten years, he wrote editorials for the *New York Age*, a prominent African American newspaper. He was one of the founders and a charter member of the American Society of Composers, Authors, and Publishers, (ASCAP) and he became field secretary for the NAACP in 1916. In 1925, he edited two authoritative volumes of spirituals for which Rosamond arranged most of the music. Five years later, he wrote *Black Manhattan*, a history of African Americans in New York, and in 1933, he wrote his autobiography, *Along This Way*. The 1900 composition "Lift Every Voice and Sing," which he wrote in collaboration with his brother Rosamond, is considered by many to be the black national anthem. James Weldon Johnson died on June 26, 1938.

WILL MARION COOK

Will Marion Cook was born in Washington, D.C., on January 27, 1869. When he was 13, he studied violin at Oberlin Conservatory where his mother had graduated in 1865. After two years at Oberlin, he left to attend the University of Berlin. While in Germany, he studied under Professor Joseph Joachim, one of the premier violinists of the era.

On his return to the United States, he studied for a brief time with Antonin Dvorak at the National Conservatory of Music, and in 1889, he made his musical debut. The following year he became the director of a chamber orchestra, and in 1893, he wrote his first composition.

His first attempt at theater was a series of skits entitled *Clorindy, or The Origin of the Cakewalk*. All the songs and the libretto were written in one ten-hour session between Cook and Paul Lawrence Dunbar. Dunbar was a well-known African American dialect poet, and when Cook's mother heard the results of their collaboration, she cried, saying, "I've sent you all over the world to study and become a great musician and you return such a nigger!"

According to Isadore Witmark, a major song publisher at the time, Cook approached him about a month before the production and told him that if he would help get *Clorindy* produced, Cook would give him publication rights to the music as well as all the royalties. Witmark agreed to help, but said that Cook could keep the royalties for himself. Cook remembered the meeting a bit differently: Witmark told him he was crazy to believe any Broadway audience would listen to Negroes sing.

During this time a new venue for entertainment emerged in New York. Previously, summer shows were not held in the city because before air conditioning, theaters were simply too hot. The innovation was to place stages on theater roofs where the air was cooler.

The Casino Theater Roof Garden was the first such open-air establishment, and for a month, Cook tried unsuccessfully to gain an audition there. In desperation, he lied to his cast, telling them that an audition was to take place the next Monday morning. When they arrived, the conductor of the roof garden's orchestra, an Englishman named John Braham, lent Cook last-minute assistance by insisting that the theater manager give Cook's troupe a chance.

The audition was successful, and they were scheduled to perform that evening. Rain canceled the first show, so they rescheduled for the following Monday. Ernest Hogan, the troupe's lead actor and a stage veteran as well as a songwriter, used the time to tighten up the performance. In the process, he dropped Dunbar's libretto, which he felt could not be heard on an uncovered roof garden at 11:00 P.M.

Clorindy, or The Origin of the Cakewalk finally opened on July 5, 1898. With a cast of 26 African Americans headed by Hogan, the operetta was a mixture of comedy, songs, and dances including the cakewalk. In some of the numbers, the performers sang and danced simultaneously, the first time this had ever been done on the stage.

The hour-long show was a triumph. Hogan's song "Who Dat Say Chicken in Dis Crowd" drew ten encores, and Cook and the cast were elated. Of the evening, Cook said:

> *I was so delirious that I drank a glass of water, thought it wine and got glorious drunk. Negroes at last were on Broadway, and there to stay….We were artists and we were going a long way. We had the world on a string tied to a runnin' red-geared wagon on a down-hill pull. Nothing could stop us, and nothing did for a decade.*

James Weldon Johnson wrote in *Black Manhattan* that Cook was "the first competent composer to take what was then known as rag-time and work it out in a musicianly way. His choruses and finales in *Clorindy*, complete novelties as they were, sung by a lusty chorus, were simply breath-taking." Even though ragtime music was not normally considered respectable because of its association with the lower class and the underworld, W. C. Handy told of hearing the hit song from *Clorindy*, "Darktown is Out Tonight," whistled in barbershops and on street corners everywhere he went.

Cook was a proud, aggressive, and angry man who, despite the success of *Clorindy* and his other musical ventures, never received the recog-

nition he felt was his due. According to Eubie Blake, "Cook was a great musician, but he tried to push things down people's throats. I think he got that in Europe. He was trying to ape Richard Wagner." A story related by Duke Ellington in *Music is My Mistress* gives more insight into Cook's character. When a reviewer of his 1895 concert in Carnegie Hall wrote that Cook was "the world's greatest Negro violinist," Cook went to see him, violin in hand:

> *"Thank you very much for the favorable review," he said. "You wrote that I was the world's greatest Negro violinist." "Yes, Mr. Cook," the man said, "and I meant it. You are definitely the world's greatest Negro violinist." With that, Dad [Ellington's nickname for him] Cook took out his violin and smashed it across the reviewer's desk. "I am not the world's greatest Negro violinist," he exclaimed. "I am the greatest violinist in the world!" He turned and walked away from his splintered instrument, and it has been said that he never picked up a violin again in his life.*

Will Marion Cook.

According to Tom Fletcher, however, Cook did play the violin at least one more time. The event took place at James Reese Europe's persuasion, when the Clef Club Orchestra played Carnegie Hall in 1912. Cook agreed to go on stage provided that he would not be introduced or asked to take a bow. Some members of the audience recognized him, and there was a tremendous response at the conclusion of his performance. The applause and cries for "speech" lasted so long that when the overcome Cook finally did try to speak, all he could do was bow.

At the turn of the century, Cook was composing popular songs, some of which were published under the name Will Marion. Later he was composer-in-chief and musical director for Williams and Walker's Broadway shows.

Cook's wife, Abbie Mitchell, was a lead singer with The Memphis Students. Her partner Tom Fletcher described her as "a singing sensation" on the troupe's European tour. She was also the female lead in Cole and Johnson's 1908 production *Red Moon* and performed with her husband's orchestra when they toured Europe in 1918. After retiring from the stage, she opened a musical and dramatic studio in New York.

Among Will Marion Cook's many frustrations was the audience's apparent desire to hear only light-hearted music from African American composers. Mary White Ovington wrote, "I am told that Mr. Cook declares that the next score he writes shall begin with ten minutes of serious music. If the audience doesn't like it, they can come in late, but for ten minutes he will do something worthy of his genius."

At the age of 49, Cook led a band called The Southern Syncopaters, also known as The New York Syncopated Orchestra, which toured Europe and gave a command performance before England's George V. It was during this tour that band member Sidney Bechet discovered the soprano sax and began to develop his technique on an instrument which was to bring him jazz greatness. After Cook returned from Europe, he led one of the Clef Club orchestras which included Paul Robeson as a vocalist.

In his autobiography, Duke Ellington, who first met Cook in the early twenties, wrote:

Several times after I had played some tune I had written but not really completed, I would say, "Now Dad, what is the logical way to develop this theme? What direction should I take?" "You know you should go to the conservatory," he would answer, "but since you won't, I'll tell you. First you find the logical way, and when you find it, avoid it, and let your inner self break through and guide you. Don't try to be anybody but yourself."

If Cook's accomplishments were hampered by his irascible nature, at least he followed his own advice: he never pretended to be anybody but himself. Will Marion Cook died in New York on July 19, 1944.

BERT WILLIAMS AND GEORGE WALKER

George Walker was born around 1873 in Lawrence, Kansas. He began his show business career as a member of a troupe of black minstrels which traveled throughout his home state. He then decided to try his luck as a solo act and worked his way west to California in medicine shows.

Egbert Williams was probably born in Antigua, the West Indies, on March 11, 1875. In 1885, his family moved to California, near Los Angeles. He attended Stanford University for a few semesters, then moved to San Francisco. There he gained experience performing in saloons, restaurants, and road shows.

Williams met Walker in San Francisco in 1893, and the pair spent two years playing different venues and putting together their act. During this time, they were employed by the Mid-Winter Exposition in Golden Gate Park to work at an exhibit of a Dahomeyan village intended to portray life in "darkest Africa." Because the real Africans were late in arriving, Williams and Walker played Dahomeyans, wearing animal skins in a setting of potted palms. Once the Dahomeyans did arrive, the duo took time to study the West African natives' singing and dancing, an experience which was to become an important influence on their work.

The two men made their way to Chicago in 1895 and tried out for Isham's Octoroons, one of the first African American companies to break from a strict minstrel format. A week later, Williams and Walker were dropped from the show. Realizing that their act wasn't working, they decided to embrace the coon stereotype, billing themselves as "The Two Real Coons." They based their act on standard minstrel routines reduced to a two-man performance: Walker played the part of a dandy and told the jokes, and Williams, dressed in mismatched, oversized clothes, played the straight man. After the audience reacted favorably to a performance in which he blackened his face, Williams donned the burnt-cork mask for the rest of his professional life.

In 1896, a musical farce called *The Gold Bug* made Williams and Walker famous. The play was weak, but the duo's performance of the cakewalk captured the audience's attention, and they soon became so closely associated with this dance that many people thought of them as its originators. After a 36-week tour with a stock company, they were booked into Koster and Bial's Music Hall in New York. Playing this well-known venue was a step up for them, and many doors opened as a result. For the next two years, Williams and Walker toured the country on the vaudeville circuit as the stars of the show. In 1897, they performed in London, but apparently the British audiences did not understand their comedic approach, and they were not well received.

Of these experiences, Williams wrote:

Long before our run terminated, we discovered an important fact: that the hope of the colored performer must be in making a radical departure from the old time "darky" style of singing and dancing. So we set ourselves the task of thinking along new lines. The first move was to hire a flat in 53rd St., furnish it, and throw our doors open....The Williams and Walker flat soon became the headquarters of all the artistic young men of our race who were stage struck....By having these men about us we had the opportunity to study the musical and theatrical ability of the most talented members of our race.

On October 11, 1901, when Williams and Walker recorded for the Victor Talking Machine Company, they became the first African American artists to record on disc. Walker's voice sounded thin on the playback, and he was not pleased. William's voice, on the other hand, was strong, and the recordings he made over the course of 20 years created a legacy of his comedic genius.

During the next few years, Williams and Walker put together a number of small productions including *A Lucky Coon, Sons of Ham*, and *The Policy Players*, but their ultimate goal was to produce and star in their own Broadway musical.

A lack of original material combined with their desire to shift focus away from the coon stereotype gave impetus to their next big step.

Remembering their job as "Dahomeyans" in San Francisco, they decided to set the scene of their next production in Africa, and in 1902, the duo teamed with Will Marion Cook, Paul Lawrence Dunbar, and Jesse Shipp to produce *In Dahomey*, the highly successful musical which allowed them to achieve their dream of performing on Broadway. Williams, now an experienced actor and a mime with incomparable timing, emerged as one of the leading comedians in the country. At the time, George Walker was quoted as saying: "My partner, Mr. Williams, is the first man I know of in our race to attempt to delineate a darky in a perfectly natural way, and I think much of his success is due to this fact."

In the spring of 1903, the team took *In Dahomey* to England. Initially, the show played to a sympathetic but not very spirited audience. However, on June 23, the tide turned after a lavish command performance at Buckingham Palace for Edward VII on the birthday of the Prince of Wales (later Duke of Windsor). The show, which ran for seven months, toured all of the British Isles and made the cakewalk fashionable in both London and Paris. On its return to New York, it played to receptive crowds at the Grand Opera House and toured for 40 weeks with performances in most major American cities.

In 1906, Williams and Walker were active in organizing an African American actors' union called The Negro's Society. That same

Bert Williams and George Walker are the "Two Real Coons" featured on this 1901 sheet.

year, they produced and starred in *In Abyssinia*, which they followed with another successful play, *Bandana Land*, in 1908.

While touring with *Bandana Land* in 1909, George Walker began to stutter and suffer memory loss, both well-known symptoms of syphilis. Over the next few years such notables as Ernest Hogan, Bob Cole, Scott Joplin, and Louis Chauvin would succumb to the same disease. Incurable at the time, it hit the ranks of African American performers so hard that by 1911, most of the small, close-knit group that had managed to bring their artistry to Broadway were dead, and it would be another 10 years before African Americans returned to the stages of Broadway. Walker died on January 8, 1911, and was buried in his Kansas hometown.

Bert Williams, without a partner for the first time in 20 years, performed in vaudeville for a while and starred in *Mr. Lode of Coal* in 1910. Later that year, Florenz Ziegfeld asked him to join the famous Follies. Williams accepted and commissioned the African American composer Will Vodery to write his songs, an association which paved the way for Vodery's engagement as arranger for the Follies from 1913 to the late 1920s.

Williams achieved great success performing in many of the Follies' productions, making as much money as the president of the United States by playing a character that could best be described as the black counterpart to Charlie Chaplin's Little Tramp. During summer breaks, he traveled to Europe and studied with the great French pantomimist Pietro, who, according to Williams, taught him that "the entire aim of art in the theater was to achieve simplicity." In 1918, Williams discussed comedy as he understood it:

All the jokes in the world are based on a few elemental ideas….Troubles are funny only when you pin them down to one particular individual. And that individual, the fellow who is the goat, must be the man who is singing the song or telling the story….It was not until I could see myself as another person that my sense of humor developed. For I do not believe there is any such thing as innate humor. It has to be developed by hard work and…I have studied it all my life.

Bert Williams' last show, considered one of his best, was *Under the Bamboo Tree*. He died on March 4, 1922, while touring with the production in Detroit. He was the original comic who never got any respect, an individual of great personal dignity who was never allowed to show it on stage. Of him, Booker T. Washington once said, "He has done more for our race than I have. He has smiled his way into people's hearts; I have been obliged to fight my way."

JAMES REESE EUROPE

Of his contemporaries, James Reese Europe's story is the saddest. He achieved much in his short life, but his greatest achievements were surely to come, and it is fair to say that the whole history of jazz would have been different had Europe not met an untimely death at the end of World War I.

James Reese Europe was born in Mobile, Alabama, on February 22, 1881. Both of his parents were musicians, and when Europe was about ten, his family moved to Washington, D.C., where he studied violin with Enrico Hurlei, the assistant director of the Marine Corps Band. Europe entered a music-writing contest at the age of 14 and was awarded second place, bested only by his sister Mary.

At 22, Europe moved to New York and began playing piano in a cabaret. He also continued his musical studies, and in 1905, he joined Joe Jordan to write for The Memphis Students. That was the year he unknowingly influenced a future songwriting great: George Gershwin remembered sitting on the curb outside Baron Wilkin's nightclub in Harlem for hours when he was seven years old, listening to Europe play.

In 1907, Europe was the musical director of Cole and Johnson's *The Shoo-Fly Regiment*. Two years later he performed the same duties for Bert Williams' *Mr. Lode Of Coal*. In 1910, he founded one of the most unusual African American organizations of the time.

The Clef Club was unique in that it was part fraternal organization and part union. The building it purchased on West 53rd Street served both as a club and as an office for bookings. Its board included William Tyers, previously an arranger for Stern Music Publishing Company, as its treasurer and assistant symphony orchestra conductor, and Henry Creamer, who would later pair with Turner Layton to write many popular songs, as its press representative and general manager. Europe was the Clef Club's first elected president as well as the conductor of its symphony orchestra.

The Clef Club Orchestra appeared at Carnegie Hall for the first time on May 2, 1912. They were so well received that they returned in 1913 and 1914. One American writer said that popular music first invaded the concert auditorium when Europe played Carnegie Hall.

One Clef Club Orchestra performance boasted 150 musicians, although it has been said that not everyone who was on stage in some shows could actually play an instrument. Some were taught just enough chords to get them through the performance, and others were simply holding instruments with rubber strings.

Nevertheless, the Carnegie Hall concerts gave the Clef Club Orchestra greater respectability among white society, and as a result, they were engaged to play at many elite functions both in New York and in London, Paris, and on yachts traveling worldwide. The club

James Reese Europe with members of the 369th Infantry Band.

functioned as a clearing house not only for musicians but also for all types of entertainers, and under Europe's leadership, it was actively involved in improving the entertainers' working conditions. Prior to this era, some establishments hired musicians primarily as waiters and bartenders who also were expected to entertain the guests. When an act was booked through the Clef Club, however, the musicians were hired solely as entertainers and received a salary, plus transportation expenses, room, and board. The club proved exceptionally successful, generating more than $100,000 a year in bookings at its height of popularity.

At the time dancing was all the rage in New York, and the most famous dancers were Vernon and Irene Castle. When the Castles met Europe at a private society party where the Clef Club Orchestra was playing, they decided to make him their band leader. They also hired black composer Ford Dabney as their musical arranger.

Europe was instrumental in the premier and success of the Castles' most famous dance creation, the fox trot, which was reputedly adapted from W. C. Handy's "The Memphis Blues." While with the Castles, he also added a saxophone to his band, giving what had previously been used mainly as a novelty in musical acts the status of a respectable jazz instrument for the first time. Europe and Dabney wrote most of the music for the Castles' dances.

In 1914, after disputes arose between Clef Club members, Europe resigned as its leader and formed the Tempo Club which, when he played for the Castles, was also called Europe's Society Orchestra. When Europe left the Castles in 1915, Ford Dabney took over his spot as band leader.

At the start of World War I, Europe enlisted as a private in the army. After passing the officer's exam, he was asked by his commander, Colonel William Hayward, to form a military band as part of the combat unit. Europe felt that it would be hard to convince New York City musicians to leave their highly paid jobs to go to war, but Colonel Hayward instructed Europe to get the musicians wherever he could. He did just that, even traveling all the way to Puerto Rico to recruit his reed players.

When the unit arrived in France on New Year's Day 1918, it was the first African American combat unit to set foot on French soil. Europe's band entertained troops and citizens in every city they visited and was received with great enthusiasm. Noble Sissle said at the time that the "Jazz germ" hit France, and it spread everywhere they went.

Throughout the war, Europe continued to write songs, composing the words to "On Patrol in No Man's Land" while hospitalized after surviving a gas attack at the front. On August 18, he was sent from the front to lead his band at an Allied conference in Paris. They were only to

play one concert, but the crowd reaction was such that both American and French officials asked them to stay in Paris for eight weeks.

During this time, Europe's group performed in a series of concerts with some of the greatest marching bands of France, Britain, and Italy. After one performance, the French band leader asked for one of Europe's arrangements so that his band could play some of this American jazz. The next day the leader questioned Europe because his band's version did not sound like the original. After listening to them play, Europe agreed and tried to explain how the jazz effect was accomplished. The puzzled Frenchman later inspected Europe's instruments; his band felt that the only explanation for the sounds they created could be that the instruments were doctored.

Europe and his band returned triumphantly to New York on February 12, 1919, and soon began a tour of American cities. The final concert on the tour was at Mechanic's Hall in Boston on May 9, 1919. That evening, when one of the "Percussion Twins," Herbert Wright, became angered by Europe's strict direction, he attacked the band leader with a knife during intermission. Noble Sissle recalled:

Jim wrestled Herbert to the ground, I shook Herbert and he seemed like a crazed child, trembling with excitement. Although Jim's wound seemed superficial, they couldn't stop

the bleeding, and as he was being rushed to the hospital he said to me: "Sissle, don't forget to have the band down at the State House at nine in the morning. I am going to the hospital and I will have my wound dressed....I leave everything for you to carry on."

Europe's jugular vein had been severed. The next day the papers carried the headlines: "The Jazz King Is Dead."

Sissle's partner Eubie Blake later said of Europe, "He was our benefactor and inspiration. Even more, he was the Martin Luther King of music." Sissle remarked:

There was only one Jim Europe, and he had not just been "made" with that band of his. There was years of experience behind that sweep of his arms, and anyone who tried to follow him would just be out of his mind....I was sure that conducting was not the field in which I was to carry on his life's dreams. In my mind his band should remain in the memory of those who heard it led by Lieutenant James Reese Europe, and that's how it ended.

Europe was buried with military honors at Arlington National Cemetery. Despite his many accomplishments, he never fulfilled his greatest ambition: to restore African Americans to the Broadway stage. It would remain for his students, Noble Sissle and Eubie Blake, to realize his dream.

ARTIST PROFILE
SHELTON BROOKS

Shelton Brooks was a member of the second generation of African American songsters, artists who came into prominence in the teens. His compositions fueled the era's dance craze and were performed by some of its best-known white singers including Nora Bayes and Al Jolson. They also were popular among the new breed of musicians who introduced jazz first to the United States and then to the world. These melodies became some of the earliest jazz standards, songs musicians knew so well that they could be played without rehearsal.

Shelton Brooks was born in Amesburg, Ontario, on May 4, 1886. When he was 15, his family moved to Detroit; his first professional job was playing piano in Cleveland.

In 1910, Sophie Tucker's maid insisted that Brooks be brought to sing for her employer in Tucker's dressing room in a Chicago vaudeville theater. It was the start of a friendship that was to enrich more than a few musical careers.

The song Brooks sang for Tucker on their first meeting was "Some of These Days," which Tucker liked and began using immediately. "I've turned it inside out," she was to write, "singing it every way imaginable, as a dramatic song, as a novelty number, as a sentimental ballad, and always audiences have loved it and asked for it." "Some of These Days," which may have been modeled on the similar tune by Frank Williams, "Some O' Dese Days," published in 1905 by the Attucks Music Publishing Company, was pub-

lished five years later by an African American-owned firm in Chicago headed by William Foster. In 1911, Brooks appeared in his first musical comedy, *Dr. Herb's Prescription, or It Happened in a Dream*. Performed in Chicago's Pekin Theater, the comedy was produced by its star, Jesse Shipp, who had previously been involved in the Williams and Walker shows in New York.

Shelton Brooks, detail from "It's Awf'ly Hard to Say Good-Bye," 1910.

Brooks quickly became known as an outstanding entertainer whose talents included singing, piano playing, and mimicking his fellow black vaudevillian Bert Williams. He also traveled as a trap drummer with Danny Small's Hot Harlem Band for several months during this period.

The second decade of the twentieth century was an era of "tango teas," where whisky, not tea, was the drink of choice, and parties that lasted till dawn, and Brooks' songs captured its moods perfectly. His 1912 publication, "All Night Long," evoked the nightclubs that literally never closed their doors; in fact, their owners often did not even have front door

keys. His 1916 instrumental called "Walkin' The Dog" inspired a dance that swept dance-mad Manhattan and the rest of the country as well.

Brooks knew how hard it was for African Americans to get their music heard, published, and eventually sung by the white stars of the day, and his own success did not blind him to the struggles of others. When he let it be known to other African American songwriters that his friend Sophie Tucker was "regular" and would do what she could to help them, among those to benefit were Noble Sissle and Eubie Blake. Their first song, "It's All Your Fault," was published in 1915 as a direct result of the Tucker-Brooks connection. This arrangement was advantageous to both Tucker and the songwriters: the new material they provided her helped the singer's career as well as their own.

At the time, New York City was said to have the best black pianists and drummers in the country, but Chicago reputedly had the best black bands. Around 1915, Brooks led a large syncopated orchestra in Chicago's Grand Theater, only one of many great African American theaters in the Windy City.

Brooks' most famous song was "Darktown Strutters' Ball." Published in 1917 and introduced to the public on record by The Original Dixieland Jazz Band, it became an instant success. The song, which may have been inspired by an actual social gathering the composer attended in San Francisco, was also recorded in 1919 by Lieutenant James Reese Europe's 369th Infantry Band.

When the first blues recordings were being made in the early twenties, Brooks became interested in this new medium. He asked Perry Bradford, who had connections in the business, to help him get a recording session. The result was a comedy record called "Darktown Court Room." The flip side carried a song by the comedy team Miller and Lyles called "You Can't Come In," and the record sold more than 80,000 copies.

During the twenties, Brooks performed in many small African American shows including *Miss Nobody From Starland* in 1920 and *K of P* in 1923. He was a prominent song-and-dance man in the show *From Dixie To Broadway*, which featured the very talented Florence Mills, who died in 1927 at the peak of her career. In the thirties, he appeared in other shows and went to Europe with Lew Leslie's *Blackbirds of 1932*. It was during this tour that he appeared in a command performance before George V.

Along with W. C. Handy and William Grant Still, the dean of black classical composers, Brooks was honored in San Francisco at the ASCAP-sponsored Festival of American Music in 1940. He died on September 6, 1975.

JOE JORDAN

Joe Jordan was a musical talent who, during the course of his long and productive life, helped to bring about several important changes in the entertainment world, and witnessed many more. He was not an actor, but his songs could turn an actor or actress into a star. And that is exactly what happened.

Jordan was born in Cincinnati, Ohio, in 1882 and studied music at the Lincoln Institute (now Lincoln University) in Jefferson City, Missouri. His name first came to light at the turn of the century when he played piano in St. Louis with Louis Chauvin and Sam Patterson. Chauvin was a brilliant ragtime pianist who favored the carefree life of a bawdyhouse piano player over a more structured and disciplined musical career, but Jordan was more ambitious. Under the guidance of Tom Turpin, a saloon owner whose piano playing was considered the best in the country at that time, Jordan formed a quartet that played in clubs and at church socials. The group was unique in that all four men—Jordan, Turpin, Chauvin, and Patterson—played piano at the same time.

Around 1900, Jordan played violin and drums in the ten-piece Taborin Band of St. Louis. In 1902, he visited New York where he and Ernest Hogan wrote the score for *Rufus Rastus*, a play starring Hogan. Hogan, who billed himself as "The Unbleached American," had written the most famous of all coon songs, "All Coons Look Alike To Me," and the play was an attempt to build on his success as the lead in Will Marion Cook's *Clorindy*.

In 1903, Patterson and Chauvin wrote the score and libretto for *Dandy Coon*, with Jordan acting as stage and musical director. Unfortunately, after a promising tryout in St. Louis, the playlet patterned after the popular Williams and Walker shows folded on the road in Des Moines.

When he was 21, Jordan moved to Chicago. The next year, he wrote the "Pekin Rag," dedicated to Bob Mott's Pekin Theater, Chicago's great African American-owned theater and first of the many such theaters and vaudeville houses that were to sprout up across the nation. The Pekin also set the stage for Chicago to become the center of the jazz world between 1915 and 1925.

In the spring of 1905, Jordan was called to New York by Ernest Hogan. Hogan had organized a group of 17 men and women—singers, dancers, and musicians—and wanted Jordan and James Reese Europe to help turn them into an all-African American ragtime orchestra and write their music. When the Memphis Students made its debut, it was the first group of its kind to play in New York City.

Up until this time, there had been no serious bands of African American musicians. The role played by Jordan, James Europe, and Ford Dabney in the organization of such groups broke new ground in the development of early orchestral jazz.

Joe Jordan (center) with members of the Memphis Students.

and orchestra leader for the Pekin in 1906 and wrote the theater's first stage production, *The Man from Bam*, with a book by Flournoy Miller and Aubrey Lyles. Jordan's band at the Pekin consisted of 16 musicians, the majority of whom were from minstrel show backgrounds. They remained the house band for the theater's comedies and vaudeville shows until 1909, with Jordan writing the music for most of their productions.

Even though he was working in Chicago, Jordan was still involved in the New York musical scene. He wrote Ada Overton Walker's "Salome Dance," which was used in a Williams and Walker production, and also wrote "That Teasin' Rag" for her in 1909. Eight years later, "That Teasin' Rag" became part of a controversy when The Original Dixieland Jazz Band used its principal strain for their tune, "Original Dixieland One-Step." After hearing a recording of it, Jordan brought legal action. The records were pulled from the shelf and relabeled with an additional credit: "Introducing 'That Teasin' Rag' by Joe Jordan."

In 1910, Jordan teamed with Will Marion Cook to write the song that made Fanny Brice a star: "Lovie Joe." According to Jelly Roll Morton, its title implied "a great lover of the ladies." Another story has it that Lovie Joe was a gambler who owned a saloon in New York before the song was written.

Fanny Brice first performed "Lovie Joe" in

The Memphis Students contained both string instruments like the banjo, mandolin, and guitar, and brass band instruments like the trumpet and saxophone; James Weldon Johnson called this "playing-singing-dancing" orchestra "the first modern jazz band ever heard on a New York stage." Later in 1905, they toured Paris, London, and Berlin under the leadership of Will Marion Cook. Solo vocalists during the first year were Tom Fletcher and Abbie Mitchell, Cook's wife.

The band was the first to sing in four-part harmony and play instruments at the same time. Their conductor, Will Dixon, also had a unique style: he danced out the rhythm across the stage as he conducted, a trick that Cab Calloway would use to thrill crowds 30 years later. Their hit songs were "Rise and Shine," "Oh, Liza Lady," "Goin' to Exit," and "Dixie Land," all by Joe Jordan.

He assumed the duties of musical director

the Ziegfeld Follies of 1910. Florenz Ziegfeld was impressed with his newly hired singer's dedication as she rehearsed it over and over again in the corner of the stage. However, his producer, Abe Erlanger, thought the song was ridiculous and the singer's interpretation and phrasing even worse, and he promptly told her so. An angry Brice informed the little man, "I live on 128th Street. It's on the edge of Harlem. They all talk that way," and walked off the stage. With that, Erlanger went into a tirade, firing her and canning "Lovie Joe."

Ziegfeld coaxed Brice back to the show, but he told her that while the song would be used on the road for the Atlantic City performance, it would be dropped for the opening in New York. Brice decided to act on her own. Instead of the dress Ziegfeld had designed for her, she found one several sizes too small, and on opening night, she sang "Lovie Joe" in blackface as planned, but wiggling back and forth to make the clinging sheath accommodate her ungainly figure. At the end of the song, she drew up the skirt, struck a knock-kneed pose, then raced off stage in mock horror. The applause was so overwhelming that the singer took eight encores. Joe Jordan, who was standing outside the theater because African Americans were not allowed inside, is said to have wept when he heard it. After Brice finally left the stage, Erlanger was the first to greet her, his broken straw hat in his hands. "See, I broke this

applauding you," he said. She kept the hat as a memento for the rest of her career.

In 1911, Jordan visited Germany with King and Bailey's Chocolate Drops. He also toured the English music halls, and between 1911 and 1913, he was back at the Pekin as musical director. He joined Will Marion Cook again in 1918, this time as financial manager and assistant director of Cook's New York Syncopated Orchestra.

When Jordan was 46, he became the conductor for *Keep Shufflin'*, a musical featuring stride pianist James P. Johnson and his best-known student, Fats Waller. The music and lyrics were composed by Henry Creamer and Andy Razaf, both of whom were active black songwriters.

Jordan was also a band leader who traveled and recorded with his group Ten Sharps and Flats. In the thirties, he directed WPA orchestras, and as a part of the week-long ASCAP Silver Jubilee Festival held in Carnegie Hall in 1939, he directed a symphony orchestra of 75 players and a 350-voice chorus. They opened the concert with Rosamond and James Weldon Johnson's rousing anthem "Lift Every Voice and Sing." During World War II, Jordan organized army bands and USO groups. Later in his career, he wrote songs with W. C. Handy and conducted the orchestra for Orson Welles' production of *Macbeth*.

Joe Jordan died at the age of 89 on September 9, 1971.

Songwriter Joe Jordan was also the musical director and orchestra leader at the Pekin Theater. The Pekin, Chicago's great black-owned theater, paved the way for similarly owned theaters and vaudeville houses across the nation and set the stage for Chicago to become the center of the jazz world between 1915 and 1925.

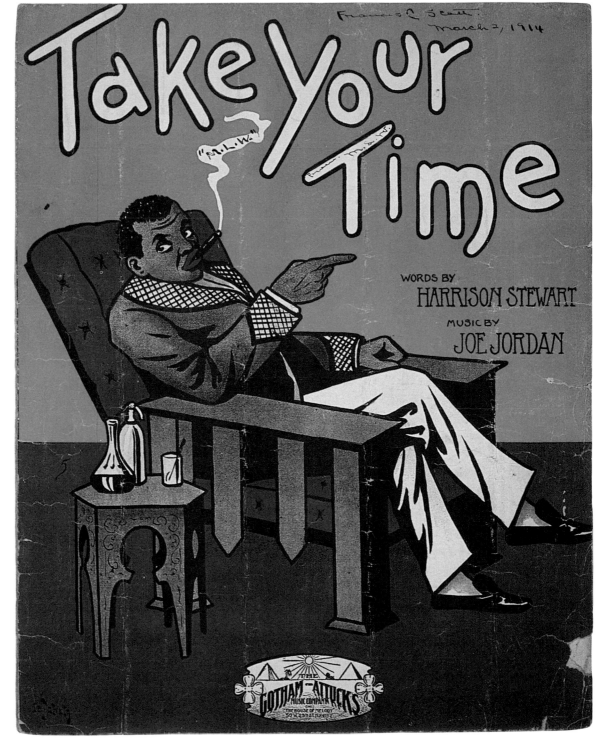

This song, the big ragtime hit of 1913, was one of the first tunes with lyrics describing a dance. Other popular dances from the period were the "Texas Tommy," developed in San Francisco by a black man named Johnny Peters, and the "Cincinnati Two-Step," which came east to New York. What the title "Ballin' The Jack" meant nobody knew, but the dance was described as a "lateral dislocation of the closely joined legs."

"The Darktown Strutter's Ball" may have been inspired by an actual social gathering Shelton Brooks attended in San Francisco. His most famous song, it was published in 1917 and introduced to the public on record by The Original Dixieland Jazz Band. It was an overnight success, recorded by at least five different groups in its first two years of existence, including Lieutenant James Reese Europe's 369th Infantry Band.

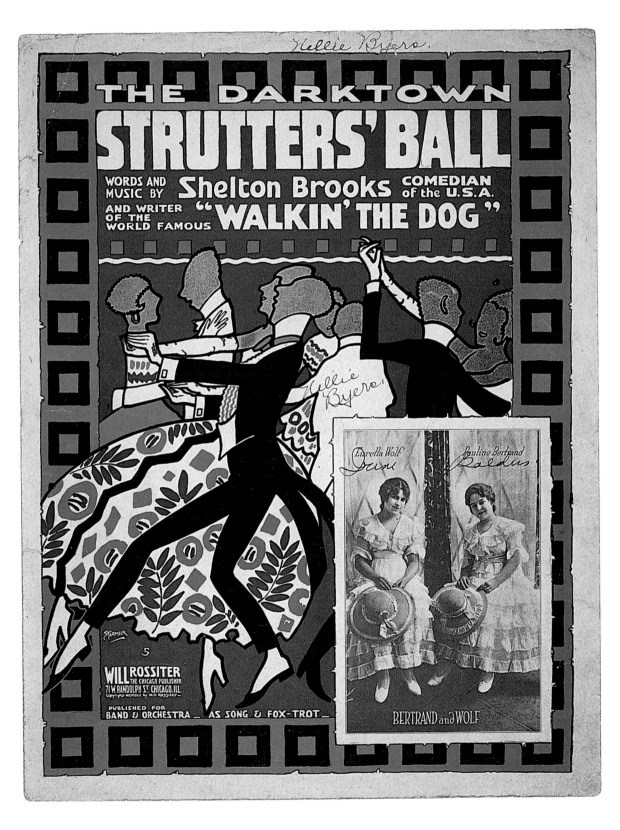

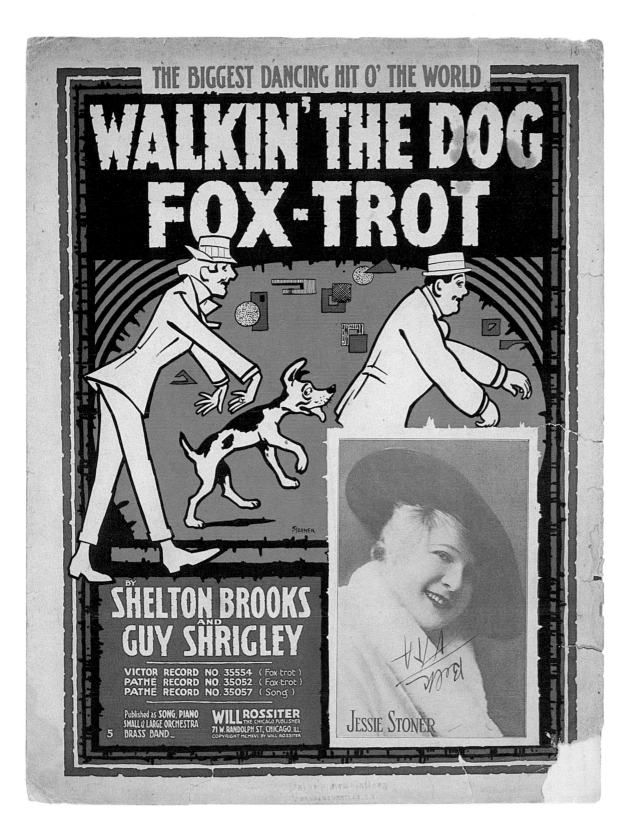

America went wild over dancing around 1912, and the trend continued for a number of years. Other popular dances with animal-related names included the "Turkey Trot," "Grizzly Bear," "Bunny Hug," "Gotham Gobble," and the "Pigeon Walk." There were also dances designed specifically to bring partners closer together than had previously been allowed, among them the "Come-To-Me Tommy," "Lover's Walk," "Hug-Me-Close," and "The Shiver."

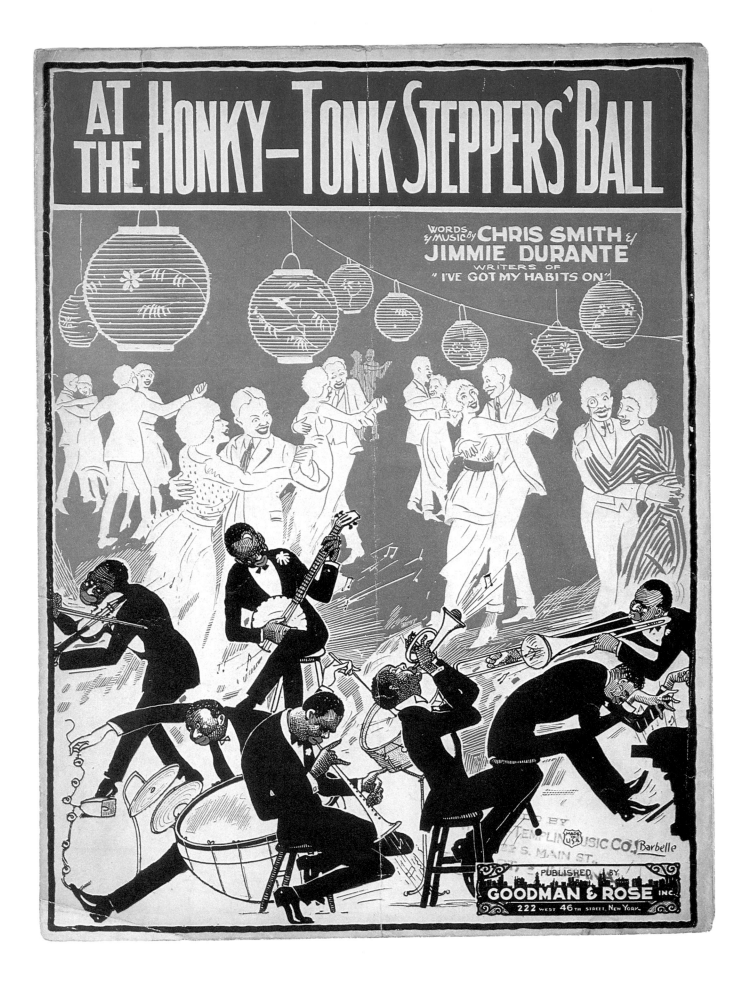

"T'AIN'T NOBODY'S BUSINESS IF I DO"

 lack popular song flourished in the post-war era known as the Jazz Age. In the process, it also influenced the course of American popular music as never before. Both jazz and blues were in full bloom; their widespread popularity among black and white musicians and audiences was unprecedented on such a large scale. Not surprisingly, the two show business enterprises most closely associated with the rise of these musical genres also grew and prospered in the 1920s; they were the TOBA vaudeville network and the record industry. In turn, the number of black vaudeville shows increased, as did the recording of black songs and musicians. At least in the initial stages of this musical boom, all concerned parties seemed to benefit from it.

The TOBA membership list was up to almost 40 theaters by 1921, when the association was taken over by a Nashville, Tennessee theater owner named Milton Starr and by Charles Turpin, brother of ragtime composer Tom Turpin and owner of a TOBA theater in St. Louis. Significantly, Turpin was one of only a handful of African American theater owners in the country.

The white entrepreneurs involved in the TOBA tended to have previous show business experience. For example, Milton Starr, the son of a Jewish immigrant, started out working in motion picture nickelodeons before owning his own theater and running the TOBA with Turpin. A few of the TOBA kingpins, such as Charles "Marse" Bailey, owner and manger of the 81 Theater on Decatur Street in Atlanta, Georgia, were ward bosses with considerable muscle in local politics and lucrative connections to the local tenderloins. One of Bailey's often-mentioned powers over his black employees was that only he could issue them the passes necessary to get through the police patrols enforcing the city's midnight curfews on African Americans.

Some of the white TOBA theater owners hired African Americans to manage and book their properties, and eventually a few of these theaters were black owned. A 1918 advertisement for the Douglas Gilmar Theater in Baltimore, Maryland, printed in that city's *Afro-American Sun*, read in part: "The only Vaudeville and Motion Picture Parlour owned and operated by colored people." Hiram Sorrell was listed as its manager and George Douglas its proprietor. The Howard Theater in Washington, D.C., was opened in 1908; although initially owned by a Jewish entrepreneur named Abe Liechman, it was managed by African Americans from the outset. Whatever the arrangement, as blacks began to migrate to the cities, urban theaters quickly emerged as the new meccas of African American entertainment.

The southern end of the TOBA circuit began in Memphis, Tennessee, where the famous Beale Street Palace Theater showcased the best-known vaudeville blues singers and jazz bands in its legendary Friday night "Midnight Rambles." Owned and operated by Italian immigrants, the Pacini brothers, the Palace had "white only" nights

Before Chris Smith came to New York City at the turn of the century, he was a performer in a medicine show in Charleston, South Carolina. The African American songwriter was at the peak of his career in the teens when he created this song with Jimmy Durante. At the time, Smith and Durante, who would collaborate on many other songs, were performing together in a vaudeville act.

at which white audiences were treated to performances by the leading black vaudeville stars. A similar arrangement was put into operation by "Marse" Bailey at the 81 Theater in Atlanta.

The TOBA crested as an entertainment enterprise in the mid-1920s, when according to the *Chicago Defender*, the network had more than 50 theaters employing hundreds of black performers who played for a weekly audience of 30,000 paying customers. Simultaneously, small communities of African American entertainers coalesced in metropolitan centers such as New York, Chicago, and Atlanta, where they organized local repertory companies. The performers were drawn to these cities by the burgeoning entertainment and recording industries, both of which were in the process of slowly opening their doors to black talent.

The heady expansion of the TOBA vaudeville network was fueled in part by a resurgence in black musical theater. The catalyst for the second wave of black musicals to hit the Broadway stage was a comedy called *Shuffle Along*, brainchild of Flournoy Miller and Aubrey Lyles, the popular Chicago-based song-and-dance team.

Miller and Lyles had formed their partnership as students at Fisk University in Nashville, Tennessee. Before migrating to Chicago, they toured the South as a minstrel act; it was during

This landmark musical was the collaborative effort of four veteran African American entertainers: Aubrey Lyles and Flournoy Miller, who wrote the book, and Noble Sissle and Eubie Blake, who wrote the music.

this period that they adopted the practice of blacking up for their routines. Along with Bert Williams, they were the only major black entertainers who continued to use blackface into the 1920s.

Working with Chicago's Pekin Stock Company, Miller and Lyles perfected their stage personas and a number of their most popular routines. One of these called "The Mayor of Dixie" became the core of *Shuffle Along*; it featured the blackface comedians portraying Steve Jenkins and Sam Peck, stage characters which would serve as the inspiration for Freeman Gosden and Charles Correll's famous "Amos and Andy" radio series launched in the late 1920s.

Miller and Lyles hired the youthful songwriting team of Noble Sissle and Eubie Blake, known on stage as "The Dixie Duo," to come up with some new songs for the show. They also lined up financial backing through their booking agent. *Shuffle Along* opened off Broadway in 1921 and was a huge box office success. It not only paved the way for a flurry of new black musicals over the next few years, but it also was responsible for beginning to break down segregation in New York theaters. For the first time ever, black patrons of African American musicals in New York City were able to attend the same show as the white patrons, although the seating sections were still segregated. *Shuffle Along* launched the careers of Florence Mills and Josephine Baker, two of the era's most glamorous black female stars.

The first two black musicals to follow

After the death of James Reese Europe in 1919, Noble Sissle and Eubie Blake were encouraged to put together an act and join the vaudeville circuit. At the time, the major vaudeville circuit only allowed one black act to perform per show. "Gee, I'm Glad That I'm from Dixie" is the song Sissle and Blake used to open their act. Even though Blake was from Baltimore and Sissle was from Indianapolis, they billed themselves as "The Dixie Duo."

Eubie Blake, Baltimore's most famous ragtime pianist, was born in that city in 1883. When his mother heard him syncopating church hymns on the family piano, she told him to "take that ragtime out of my house." According to Blake, it was the first time he knew what he had been playing was called ragtime.

Shuffle Along were financial disasters. Both were produced on shoe-string budgets by black songwriters. *Put and Take* was put together by Perry Bradford, Spencer Williams, Tim Brymn, and Irving Miller, Flournoy Miller's brother. Set in a northern city and featuring contemporary black characters, the show was panned by the critics and forced to close after a few weeks. A similar fate derailed *Strut Miss Lizzie*, a musical produced and written by the talented team of Henry Creamer and Turner Layton. Even though the show contained two of their most popular songs, "Dear Old Southland" and "Way Down Yonder in New Orleans," it failed to attract an audience and was forced to close in debt.

This trend continued into the next year. *Oh Joy* (1922), an African American-produced musical starring Ethel Waters, which did well in Boston, went bankrupt during its short Broadway run. Noble Sissle and Eubie Blake, who had parted company with Miller and Lyles in a dispute over the ownership rights to *Shuffle Along*, produced their own Broadway musical, *Chocolate Dandies*, in 1924. It was panned by the New York critics and closed after a brief run.

In contrast, the black musicals produced during this same period by white show business impresarios like Lew Leslie and George White, Broadway insiders who could afford more lavish productions and larger promotion budgets, were major box office hits. Leslie staged his first black musical, *Plantation Revue*, on Broadway in 1922. The show featured an array of African American talent, including bandleader and arranger Will Vodery, songwriter Shelton Brooks as the master of ceremonies, and Florence Mills as the star attraction. After a successful Broadway run, the musical was revamped as *From Dixie to Broadway* for a European tour which made Florence Mills into an international star. This second version of the show returned to New York in 1924, and embarked on another profitable Broadway run.

Leslie went on to produce a string of successful black musicals for the Broadway stage known as the "Blackbird" revues. They included *Blackbirds of 1928*, which featured Adelaide Hall as the female lead singing "I Can't Give You Anything But Love" and his newest discovery, veteran tap dancer Bill "Bojangles" Robinson. Another show in the series, *Blackbirds of 1930*, showcased Ethel Waters singing the songs of pianist Eubie Blake and lyricist Andy Razaf, including the risque hit "My Handy Man Ain't Handy No More."

The other leading white impresario of black musicals in the 1920s was George White, the Broadway veteran who staged the famous "Scandals" vaudeville revues early in the decade. White

The team of Dorothy Fields and Jimmy McHugh wrote songs for a number of Lew Leslie's productions that featured African Americans, including the early Cotton Club Revues.

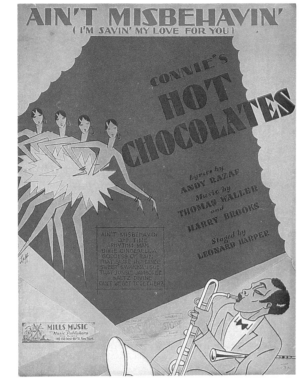

Fats Waller's composition, "Ain't Misbehavin'," which served as his trademark, was written in 1929 for the show *Hot Chocolates*.

produced *Running Wild* (1924) as a showcase for Miller and Lyles, billed as "America's Foremost Colored Comedians." He hired lyricist Cecil Mack and pianist James P. Johnson to write the music for the show, and one of their songs, the "Charleston," helped launch the popular dance craze of the same name. White staged two additional black musical revues featuring Miller and Lyles, *Rang Tang* (1927) and *Keep Shufflin'* (1928). Like Leslie, his Broadway shows were always a financial success.

The end of the decade brought another flurry of black-produced musicals to the Broadway stage, the most prominent of which were *Bottomland* (1927), *Messin' Around* (1929), *Deep Harlem* (1929), and *Hot Chocolates* (1929). *Bottomland*

was written and produced by Clarence Williams as a vehicle for his songs and his vaudeville trio, which included himself on piano accompanying vocalists Eva Taylor, who was Williams' wife, and Sara Martin. *Messin' Around*, written and produced by songwriters Perry Bradford and James P. Johnson, featured an on-stage female prize fight inserted as a last-ditch gambit to save the show from a quick demise. *Deep Harlem* was an ambitious musical history of African Americans from ancient Africa to contemporary Harlem. With songs written by Joe Jordan and Henry Creamer, the show was an outgrowth of the artistic and musical ferment associated with the famous Harlem Renaissance, which was in full swing at the time. *Hot Chocolates* showcased the piano and songwriting talents of "Fats" Waller and featured two of his most popular songs, "Ain't Misbehavin'" and "Black and Blue," written in conjunction with lyricist Andy Razaf, an expatriate tribal prince from Madagascar. George Immerman, owner of the Harlem nightclub known as Connie's Inn where Waller was a star attraction, bankrolled the show, which was essentially a version of the musical revue developed around Waller in Immerman's club.

Perhaps because they were produced late in the decade during a period of general economic decline and had minimal financial backing, all of these black musicals failed to become box office hits and closed after a short period of time. Nevertheless, they still managed to help establish the black musical, and by extension black popular song, as a fixture on Broadway.

This song was written in 1918 by African American songsters Henry Creamer and Turner Layton. For the next two years, it was a number-one and number-two hit for three of the most popular singers of the era: Henry Burr and Albert Campbell's duet and Marian Harris' single. It was revived in 1927, when Sophie Tucker's version was topped on the charts by Bessie Smith's. In the thirties, it emerged as a jazz classic.

In 1917, African American songwriters Henry Creamer and Turner Layton were just starting their careers; they went on to produce a great number of popular songs including "Way Down Yonder in New Orleans" and "Dear Old Southland." Later Layton worked as a singer in English music halls, and Creamer collaborated with James P. Johnson to write "If I Could Be with You One Hour Tonight."

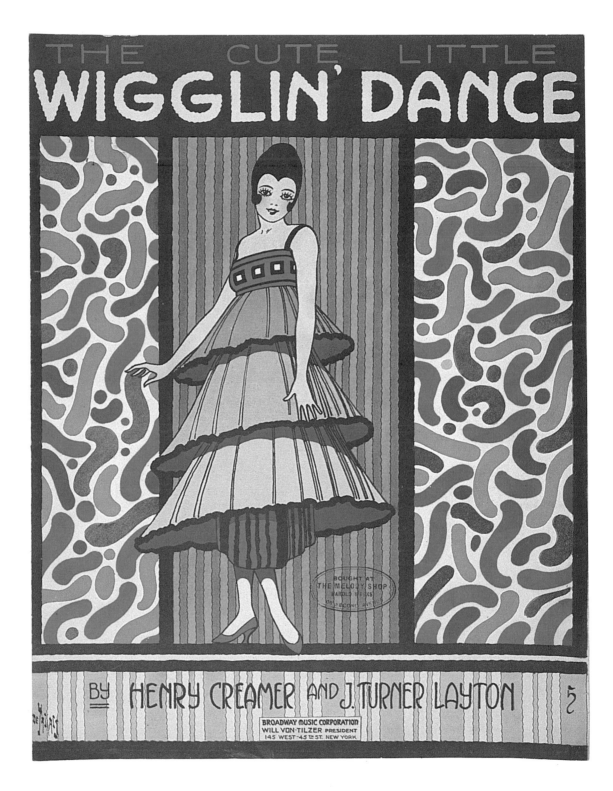

By the end of World War I, Tin Pan Alley's major publishing firms had moved from the 28th Street location to the Broadway theater district, where vaudeville productions showcased their songs. With help from ASCAP, Tin Pan Alley also consolidated its hold on the music industry in New York. The 15 largest ASCAP-member publishing firms produced up to 90 percent of the commercial songs coming off the Tin Pan Alley assembly line.

At first, ASCAP royalties were distributed equally among composers, lyricists, and publishers, and the music users targeted for collection were local hotels and cabarets featuring live music, as well as the record companies. In 1920, ASCAP instituted a new royalty policy giving half to the publishers and half to the composers and lyricists. Its revamped board of directors reflected this change: publishers now constituted 50 percent of the board membership, and the other 50 percent was made up of composers and lyricists. Moreover, the music-users list was expanded to include motion picture companies and radio stations. At this stage in its development, ASCAP had already evolved into the most powerful trade organization in the industry. Among its clients were the country's most prestigious tunesmiths and largest publishing firms.

In spite of the groundswell of interest in black popular music after World War I, ASCAP's growing membership roll remained predominantly white. By 1920, there were only ten African Americans in the organization, but many more were knocking on the door as Tin Pan Alley attracted increasing numbers of black songwriters hoping to benefit from the boom in jazz and blues.

Some of the best-known African American tunesmiths based in New York City during the 1920s were W. C. Handy, Bessie Smith, Clarence Williams, Perry Bradford, Eubie Blake, Alberta Hunter, J. Rosamond Johnson, Henry Creamer, James P. Johnson, Porter Grainger, Cecil Mack, Shelton Brooks, and Spencer Williams. Many of the men in this group, like W. C. Handy and Clarence Williams, also established their own publishing firms to collect all the royalties on the songs they wrote.

Black songwriters tended to be more respectful of their musical heritage than their white counterparts and drew many of their themes, lyrics, melodies, and song structures from the black oral tradition. This was especially the case when the composer was from the South and was personally familiar with the African American folklore and folk music there. As Clarence Williams stated in an interview with a noted black music scholar, "Why, I'd never have written blues if I had been white. You don't study to write blues, you feel them."

W. C. Handy's approach to musical composition also relied heavily on his own experiences and first-hand exposure to African American folksongs. In his autobiography, he described how he went about writing his first commercial hit, "Mr. Crump," which he later retitled "The Memphis Blues":

Detail of W. C. Handy from "Loveless Love," 1921.

One of the first blues ever published, "The Memphis Blues" was labeled a "southern rag" on the cover to make it appeal to a larger audience.

Perry "Mule" Bradford was another important black songwriter who used southern folk material in his compositions. Born in Montgomery, Alabama, in 1895, he spent much of his youth in Atlanta, Georgia, where his family moved in 1902. The Bradfords initially lived in a house next to the Fulton Street Jail. In the evening, the jail's black inmates would pass the time singing blues and other folk songs. This was where young Perry first heard the music that would soon become his livelihood.

Like Handy and Williams, Bradford became an interpreter and a popularizer of black folk music, especially the blues. In his autobiography, he cited two different songs that he used in his repertoire by writing down their lyrical cores. Both were well-known folk blues:

The melody of "Mr. Crump" was mine throughout. On the other hand, the twelve bar, three line form of the first and third strains, with its three chord basic harmonic structure (tonic, subdominant, dominant seventh) was already used by Negro roustabouts, honky tonk piano players, wanderers, and others of their underprivileged but undaunted class from Missouri to the Gulf, and had become a common medium through which any such individual might express his personal feelings in a sort of musical soliloquy. My part in their history was to introduce this, the "blues" form, to the general public, as the medium for my own feelings and my own musical ideas.

Baby you don't know my mind, no-no-no
My gal quit me and treated me so unkind
so when you see me laughing now
I'm only laughing just to keep from crying.

My gal walked the street till she got
 soaking wet
And this is what she said to every
 man she met
Don't want your dollars, just give
 me a lousy dime
So I can feed that hungry man of mine.

The second was a variation on a song that Jelly Roll Morton also used in his repertoire, crediting it

BEALE STREET
ANOTHER MEMPHIS "BLUES"
BY
W. C. HANDY

Published by PACE & HANDY MUSIC CO. Memphis, Tenn.

5

"HOME OF THE BLUES"

W. C. Handy wrote and published this song in 1917. Beale Street was the center of black life in Memphis in the early 1900s. Note that the marching band represents Handy's own group. "PWees," the business on the right, indicates the favorite hangout where Handy wrote many of his songs, including the "St. Louis Blues."

Perry Bradford was an African American songster and singer who went by the nickname "Mule." His most famous composition was "You Can't Keep a Good Man Down;" his "Crazy Blues" was the first blues song ever recorded by a black woman. During the twenties, he recorded with such jazz greats as Louis Armstrong, James P. Johnson, and Buster Bailey.

to Mamie Desdoumes, the first New Orleans singer to be identified with the blues. The folk nature of these traditional blues, which were popular before the emergence of the record industry, allowed many individuals to have their own personal versions of songs prominent in the oral tradition. With the advent of copyright laws and commercial recordings, this became more difficult.

After World War I, the record labels continued to favor recording white entertainers' "cover" versions of black popular songs over producing African American renditions of the same material. Covering was a frequently used technique designed to introduce the popular music of a smaller subculture to the audience of a larger cultural group. In this instance, its purpose was both to entice a curious white public to purchase recordings of the new black music and to "upgrade" it.

Upgrading was synonymous with commercializing; it attempted to bring African American music more in line with European musical conventions, while superimposing upon it a veneer of bourgeois Anglo-American respectability. The net result was that a significant percentage of the blues and jazz recorded in the teens and twenties was drained of its African American characteristics and working-class content. This diluting process and the technical constraints inherent in the early recording process, like fidelity and the length of a disc, converged to stifle somewhat both authenticity and innovation in black popular music.

The Victor label's first jazz and blues re-

leases by white entertainers, issued in 1917, included two discs destined to be among the biggest commercial hits of the era. The hit record in the blues category was Sophie Tucker's version of W. C. Handy's classic "St. Louis Blues," which sold over a million copies. In the jazz category, the Original Dixieland Jazz Band's (ODJB) first release, "Livery Stable Blues," also sold over a million copies.

The ODJB was a group of five young white musicians from New Orleans who had been inspired by the burgeoning "hot" ensemble style of jazz in vogue among that city's black working class while they were growing up. The group's first national booking was in Chicago in 1916. Several months later, the band moved on to New York, and within a matter of weeks their popularity soared. The new hot music they played became the rage

The Original Dixieland Jazz Band and the New Orleans Rhythm Kings were two white groups which capitalized on the growing interest in jazz in the teens.

of the city, and they were immediately signed to record for the Victor label. "Livery Stable Blues" was a jazz novelty tune featuring cornet and trombone barnyard imitations of cows and horses, and the minstrel mentality it suggests may have accounted for the band's stylized, self-conscious approach to this new genre. The spectacular success of the ODJB was one of the catalysts that launched the Jazz Age for a youthful "lost generation" of white artists, musicians, writers, and radical intellectuals. The music came to symbolize the rebellious spirit of the fabled Roaring Twenties.

The song "Happy Feet" was used in a 1930 Technicolor movie musical called *The King of Jazz* featuring Paul Whiteman.

The most successful white cover artists of the period included vocalists Sophie Tucker, Gene Austin, Al Jolson, Rudy Vallee, and Hoagy Carmichael, as well as bandleaders Paul Whiteman, Ben Pollack, Ben Bernie, Jean Goldkette, and Vincent Lopez. Whiteman, the self-proclaimed "King of Jazz," was the era's best-known white jazz musician. A classically trained violinist, he formed his own "symphonic jazz" dance band to capitalize on the music's sudden popularity. His large orchestra owed more to modern European musical conventions than to the hot improvisational New Orleans jazz style of black musicians, but he was able to define the music on his own terms, and to convince a naive white public that it was the real thing. To his credit, Whiteman did employ a number of talented white jazz musicians like trumpeter Bix Beiderbecke, and he helped to create a more favorable climate for the acceptance of jazz by the American public. This paved the way for the recording and eventual recognition of the pivotal black jazz giants of the era, such as King Oliver, Louis Armstrong, Jelly Roll Morton, Sidney Bechet, Coleman Hawkins, Earl Hines, Fletcher Henderson, and Duke Ellington.

The first show business entrepreneur to talk a record company into recording a blues composition by a black female vocalist backed up by a black jazz band was Perry Bradford, who was himself an African American. Bradford argued that "fourteen million Negroes will buy records if recorded by one of their own," and one of his pet projects was to convince a leading record company that this was true. The two major labels, Victor and Columbia, turned Bradford down. A smaller label called Okeh agreed to record a few of his songs, but only if they were sung by Sophie Tucker. When previous commitments made it impossible for Tucker to do the session, Bradford's original choice, Mamie Smith, was given the nod.

After an undistinguished first release, Mamie Smith and Her Jazz Hounds recorded "Harlem Blues" on the Okeh label in 1920. A

When he Plays Jazz he's Got —

HOT LIPS

(A Blues Fox Trot Song)

Words and Music by
Henry Busse
Henry Lange and
Lou Davis

This was the theme song of Henry Busse, who helped write it. Busse was a white, German-born trumpet player in Paul Whiteman's Band. After Whiteman's historic premiere of George Gershwin's "Rhapsody in Blue," he became known as the "King of Jazz." Many famous jazzmen passed through the ranks of this band, including Joe Venuti, Eddie Lang, Bix Beiderbecke, and the Dorsey Brothers.

African American songster Spencer Williams had a hand in writing a number of popular songs including "Royal Garden Blues," "I Found a New Baby," and "Everybody Loves My Baby." In 1925, he put together a show intended for the Paris stage called "The Revue Negre," which launched the career of a rising young star named Josephine Baker. Later in life, Williams produced films and made his home in Sweden.

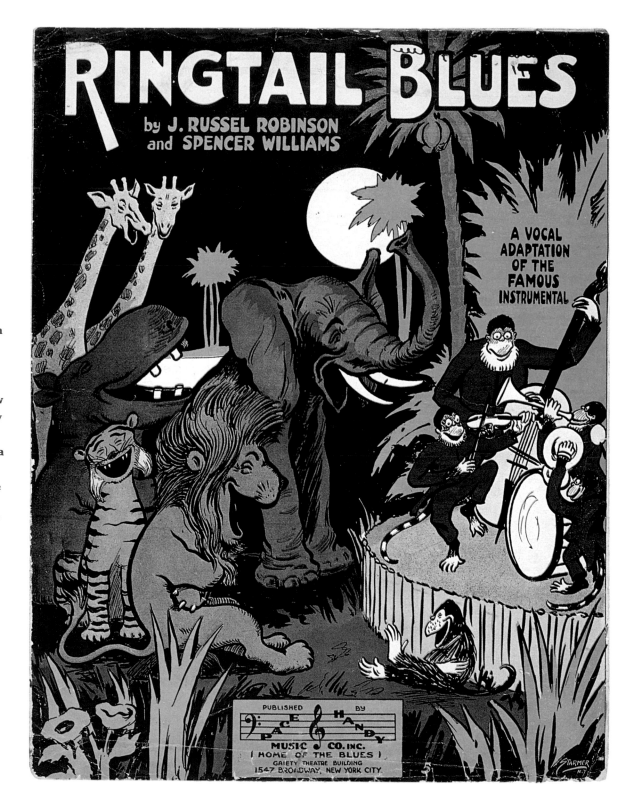

Handy published this song in New York City after he moved his company there from Memphis. Whatever his own feelings might have been about such harsh images of African Americans, he used them on his covers because they were what sold music. Handy and his partner Harry Pace were not only in the sheet music business in the early twenties. They also started the Black Swan Record Company, one of the first black-owned recording companies.

number that she was singing regularly in a local black musical revue called "Made in Harlem," the song was Bradford's revision of one he had learned in 1912 called "Nervous Blues." To avoid a possible copyright suit by the backers of "Made in Harlem," the title was changed to "Crazy Blues."

"Crazy Blues" was an unprecedented success. Proving that Bradford's assessment had been correct, it opened the floodgates for the rush to record black popular song, especially the blues. The recording also jump-started the career of Mamie Smith, who went on to become one of the decade's most popular black female vocalists.

Okeh Records sold about 75,000 copies of "Crazy Blues" in the first month after its release, and surpassed the 200,000-mark during its first year in the record stores. According to his own records, Perry Bradford received close to $20,000 in royalties. Given the sales figures, this was considerably less than that to which he was legally entitled. At the time, it was difficult to collect royalties from the record labels because they were the ones who kept tabs on how many discs were sold. To maximize their profits, they attempted to buy the copyrights to the songs they recorded. Failing to do that, they would offer contracts that paid the copyright holders only a percentage of the royalty monies. It was in this manner that Okeh initially pressured Bradford to waive his royalty rights to "Crazy Blues," but his response was: "Please be advised that the only thing Perry Bradford waives is the American flag!"

Perry Bradford not only ran his own music publishing firm, he also was instrumental in the introduction of African American musicians on commercial radio.

In the wake of Okeh's success with "Crazy Blues," blues and jazz recordings were made by a number of newly formed independent companies including Arto, Emerson, Gennett, Perfect, Pathe, Ajax, Vocalion, and Paramount. However, only a few of these labels managed to survive the decade—promotion and distribution problems usually caused their early demise.

A handful of black-owned record companies were also launched in the 1920s, only to meet a fate similar to that of the small white-owned labels. W. C. Handy and his partner Harry Pace founded the Black Swan Record Company in 1921. The label reported more than $100,000 in sales during its first year of operation, but three years later it was in serious debt, and the owners were forced to sell the company to Paramount Records. Other black-owned labels included the Sunshine label, based in Los Angeles; Merritt Records, based in Kansas City; and Mayo "Ink" Williams' Black Patti label in Chicago. All folded after a year or two.

Even the two dominant companies, Columbia and Victor, which jumped on the blues and jazz bandwagon when it became apparent that a new African American market for discs did in fact exist, were experiencing financial trouble due to the advent of commercial radio. Columbia's sales plummeted from $7 million in profits to a loss of $4.5 million, forcing the company to file for bankruptcy in 1923. Victor's sales declined from $51 million to $25 million between 1921 and 1925.

In general, though, the smaller record labels

were at a considerable disadvantage. Unlike the major recording companies, they couldn't afford to advertise extensively on a national level, and they had no means of distributing their discs beyond their local bases of operation. As a result, they invariably went out of business, while the larger companies, despite their economic difficulties, were able to buy up the smaller labels and take over new markets. This was especially true for the black record companies, which never gained a foothold in the record business, even in that section of it oriented toward black consumers. The economic structure of the industry, coupled with its racial policies and standards, ultimately proved to be insurmountable obstacles.

Okeh, Columbia, and Paramount emerged as the leaders in the recording of black music. The pacesetter was Okeh, and by 1923, the label had released 40 discs by black artists: six jazz instrumentals, 11 religious records, and 23 blues recordings.

At first, Okeh advertised this material as "Colored" records and grouped them together in a "Colored Catalogue." In 1922, however, the label placed advertisements in the *Chicago Defender* for "Race phonograph stars" and Okeh "race records." Within a year, the company had dropped the word "colored" from its advertising. Ralph Peer, the man who supervised the label's black releases, would later take credit for coining the term "race record." However, it is more than likely that he adopted it from the *Chicago Defender*, which frequently used

"race" as a progressive designation for African Americans. "Race" was symbolic of black pride and solidarity in the 1920s, and it was usually favored over "colored" or "Negro" by African Americans in the urban North. Peer did not want to offend black consumers, which is probably why he made the switch in the first place. In any event, soon thereafter the term "race records" was being used by all of the other record labels that sold discs by black artists.

Columbia Records' ascent in the race record market was stimulated by its exclusive recording contract with Bessie Smith, the highly acclaimed "Empress of the Blues." Smith's agent with Columbia was Clarence Williams, who negotiated her first

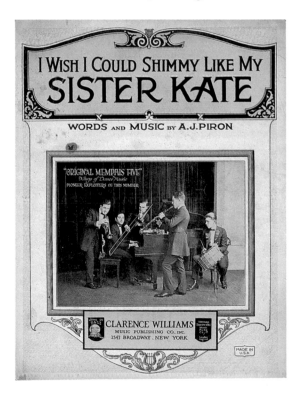

The song's black composer, Armand Piron, was born in New Orleans in 1888. His society group, which primarily played stock arrangements, made him one of that city's most successful orchestra leaders.

New Orleans-born Clarence Williams wrote songs that were popular across the United States. He was an entrepreneur who had his own publishing companies in both New Orleans and New York City and owned three music stores in Chicago when he lived there. Williams was adept at all sides of the music business from writing, publishing, and performing to managing other artists.

contract with the label in 1923. Williams worked as a talent scout for Frank Walker, supervisor of Columbia's race record operation. He also owned his own music publishing firm. He negotiated a contract for $125 per title plus a percentage of the royalties. However, all of the royalties from Columbia went to Williams' firm, and Smith received only half of the recording fee per title. When she discovered the full implications of the deal, Smith fired Williams and renegotiated her contract directly with Walker.

The second time around, although Smith got all of her $125 fee per selection plus a $1,500 guarantee per year, Walker dropped the royalty clause from her contract. This enabled him to copyright her songs for Columbia and his own music publishing firms, Frank Music Company and later Empress Music, Inc. As a result, Walker collected half the royalty fees and Columbia got the other half. This was a common business practice among race record entrepreneurs. Publishing firms like Walker's and the two Ralph Peer set up, Southern Music Publishing Company and Peer International Corporation, allowed record executives to take full advantage of their strategic positions in the music industry for their employers' and their own financial benefit.

Over a ten-year period, Bessie Smith recorded 160 selections for the Columbia race label, 38 of which were copyrighted in her name. Although her record sales officially averaged more than 20,000 discs, some of her biggest hits sold up to 800,000 discs in their first six months. Given these figures, she easily made more than a million dollars for Columbia during her recording career. Yet Smith never got any royalty monies for her efforts. In all probability, like many other race recording artists, she knew nothing about the copyright laws. Columbia paid her $28,575.

Walker made a fortune on his music publishing business, and the previously bankrupt Columbia label was prosperous enough by 1925 to purchase the patents necessary to introduce electrically recorded discs to the general public. A year later, Columbia bought out Okeh, one of its chief competitors.

In 1926, the record business reached a high-water mark in sales—$128 million—a figure the industry would not surpass until after World War II. The market for race records also mushroomed, and it was estimated that by 1925, African Americans were buying six million discs a year. These figures were based on data from only the top three race record labels, which suggests that the sales were in fact somewhat higher.

The number of race record releases peaked in 1928, when the yearly total reached the 500-mark. Even latecomers like the Victor label were now devoting a significant portion of their catalogs to this material; more than 20 percent of Victor's 1928 releases were race records. Along with the blues and jazz musicians being recorded in New York, the leading race labels were also now recording African American musicians in the South.

Detail of the logo for Clarence Williams' New York publishing company from "I Wish I Could Shimmy Like My Sister Kate," 1922.

Paramount was the first record company to take full advantage of the wealth of southern-based black musicians and vocalists. The label, which had been founded by the Wisconsin Chair Company in 1917 as an outgrowth of its phonograph manufacturing business, launched its race record series in New York in 1922.

Two years later, Paramount established a second race recording base in Chicago and hired Mayo "Ink" Williams to supervise the operation there. By that time Chicago had a large black ghetto and a thriving red-light district. This translated into jobs for black musicians who migrated to the city in large numbers, especially from the Mississippi Delta and New Orleans.

Ink Williams' nickname stemmed from his ability to sign talented black performers to contracts for Paramount. Shortly after he was hired, he signed up two of the most popular female blues singers on the black vaudeville circuit, Ma Rainey and Ida Cox. Rainey recorded 93 titles for Paramount in the 1920s, one-third of which were listed as her own compositions, but like Bessie Smith, she received no royalty monies. The publisher for her releases was the Chicago Music Publishing Company, set up by Williams to file for copyrights to all the race material he recorded for Paramount.

Ink Williams also signed and recorded Blind Blake and Blind Lemon Jefferson, two of the South's best-known rural bluesmen. Blind Blake was the mercurial blues bard who pioneered the Piedmont ragtime guitar style. Born in Florida, he spent his early youth in Georgia before becoming a vagabond blues musician. His travels took him as far north as Chicago, where he was discovered by Williams. He was hired as a studio musician for Paramount in 1926 and worked there intermittently for the next five years. During this period, he also recorded 80 titles on his own for the label. It is highly unlikely that Blake was paid any royalties for his songs, even though they were a commercial success. Blind, illiterate, and alcoholic, he was extremely vulnerable to exploitation. As a result, he was habitually given a bottle of liquor for each recording session and paid a flat fee for his efforts.

Blind Lemon Jefferson, the legendary Texas blues oracle, recorded 75 songs for Paramount between 1926 and 1930. He was brought to the label's attention by a Dallas, Texas talent scout, and proved to be the best-selling rural bluesman of the decade. Jefferson was credited as the composer of 31 of his recorded titles, but like Blake, he probably received a flat fee for the selections he recorded and no royalty monies. The unfamiliarity of these rural blues musicians with copyright laws, coupled with their illiteracy and the custom of providing them with free liquor at recording sessions, made them particularly susceptible to the chicanery of race record executives like Williams.

The successful marketing of rural blues discs was the catalyst for an upsurge in field recording ventures to southern cities by the race record companies. The trend was launched by

Harlem was the center of cultural activity for African Americans in the twenties when blacks from across America and the Caribbean migrated to this oasis in the middle of Manhattan. The movement in literature and the arts which resulted from this influx was later known as the Harlem Renaissance. The twenties also saw further developments in jazz led by Fletcher Henderson, Duke Ellington, and their orchestras.

Ralph Peer in the early 1920s while he was still with Okeh. At the urging of Polk Brockman, a white furniture store owner who also worked as an Okeh talent scout, Peer took a unit to Atlanta, Georgia, to record local blues artists there. He moved over to the Victor label in the middle of the decade and continued to organize field recording expeditions, becoming the first race record entrepreneur to record a number of popular southern blues musicians like Blind Willie McTell, Tommy Johnson, Furry Lewis, the Memphis Jug Band, and Gus Cannon and his Jug Stompers.

By the mid-1920s, the development of portable electric recording equipment made field recording sessions both more feasible and more profitable. In addition to Victor and Okeh, the Columbia, Vocalion, and Gennett race labels also sent field recording units to such major southern cities as Atlanta, New Orleans, Memphis, Dallas, Birmingham, and Jackson, Mississippi.

Generally, the rural blues musicians who made commercial recordings during these field trips were paid much less than their vaudeville blues and jazz counterparts. For example, Columbia paid Georgia blues pioneer Peg Leg Howell $15 a selection at the same time that Bessie Smith was making $200 a title. Royalty fees for these rural blues performers were habitually excluded from their contracts. In fact, Ralph Peer and the others who followed him undertook the field recording ventures primarily to find new songs to copyright for their own publishing firms and record labels.

As jazz and blues evolved from their southern folk roots to achieve national fame and fortune in the post-war period, a new genre of African American sacred song known as "gospel" was making its debut. Up until this time, black religious song had been dominated by the spirituals. In addition to the ongoing popularity of jubilee choral groups like the Fisk Jubilee Singers and the Hampton Jubilee Singers, the early 1900s also witnessed the rise of a new breed of composers and performers who devoted a good deal of their time and talent to the presentation of traditional spirituals in concert hall settings; they included Roland Hayes, William Grant Still, James Weldon Johnson, and a young Paul Robeson. But simultaneously, gospel songs were also beginning to take root and grow.

In essence, gospel songs were spirituals with a modern beat and, in many cases, instrumental accompaniments. From its inception, this new religious music was deeply influenced by the ragtime, blues, and jazz of the era. The lyrics to the songs were more upbeat and optimistic than those of the spirituals. Gospel songs were the bearers of "good news," suggesting that religious salvation and happiness were achievable in this world as well as in the next.

By the 1920s, gospel was the dominant religious music among the black Baptist, Holiness, Sanctified, and Pentecostal denominations in both the South and the North. In 1921, the National Baptist Convention published an official hymnal entitled *Gospel Pearls*, which contained 160 songs and soon became the best-known black gospel songbook in the country.

The most important gospel composer of the decade was Thomas A. Dorsey, who began his musical career as a bluesman. Dorsey was a studio pianist and songwriter for Ink Williams at Paramount Records in Chicago before his dramatic religious conversion following his wife's tragic death. He initially wrote blues songs for, and recorded with, some of the era's greatest blues performers including Ma Rainey and Tampa Red, the talented guitarist who co-authored with him the risque blues hit "It's Tight Like That." After his religious conversion, Dorsey devoted his life to gospel music and his church. His best-known gospel compositions were "We Will Meet in the Sweet By and By," "Precious Lord Take My Hand," and "Peace in the Valley."

The advent of gospel music would have far-reaching consequences for the evolution of black popular song, both sacred and secular, in the years ahead. Its variety and vitality particularly inspired the next generation of African Americans growing up in the black church, individuals who would go on to achieve important musical landmarks as composers and performers. Most of these second-generation gospel greats, like Mahalia Jackson, Roberta Martin, Clara Ward, Archie Brownlee, and R.H. Harris, sang only religious material in public. But others like the Golden Gate Jubilee Quartet and Sister Rossetta Tharpe also performed and recorded secular numbers. They set the stage for the illus-

trious careers of Dinah Washington, Ray Charles, Aretha Franklin, and Sam Cooke in the post-World War II era.

All of these artists received their musical training in the black church before moving on to the world of commercial show business. Needless to say, the popular music that they have been associated with over the years was deeply influenced by their gospel foundations. Everything from rhythm and blues to doowop to soul and ultimately even to rap has roots in gospel somewhere along the way. Its importance to black popular song has steadily increased as the century has progressed.

The 1920s also proved to be a golden age in the evolution of jazz. At the onset of the decade, the music reached a highwater mark in popularity among black musicians and urban audiences. It had already subsumed ragtime as both a separate style and a commercial genre and had crossed over into the mainstream of American popular song, with help from white cover versions. It now appealed across both race and class lines.

White cover versions of jazz continued to be recorded by the music industry, but now they were complemented by black jazz groups on disc. Kid Ory and his band initiated the recording of jazz on the race record labels in 1922, with his release of "Society Blues." A year later, another New Orleans jazz ensemble, Joe "King" Oliver's Creole Jazz Band, recorded a definitive series of standards from the cradle of jazz, including "Room Rent Blues" and "Dipermouth Blues." Oliver's

Detail of a Charleston dancer from "Brown Sugar," 1926.

Maceo Pinkard was a prolific black song-writer whose most famous compositions were "Sweet Georgia Brown" and "Gimme a Little Kiss, Will Ya Huh?" Sophie Tucker was but one of the many well-known white singers to perform his works. Between 1890 and 1954, only 12 songs were recorded more times than "Sweet Georgia Brown."

band used arrangements from a common pool of songs and solo improvisation; it also featured two of New Orleans' most promising newcomers, Johnny Dodds on clarinet and Louis Armstrong on cornet.

In the mid-1920s, Armstrong, who was destined to become the most important jazz innovator of the pre-World War II era, made a classic series of recordings for the Columbia label, referred to as the "Hot Five" or "Hot Seven" discs. The best-known releases were "West End Blues," "Basin Street Blues," "Big Butter and Egg Man," and "Struttin' with Some Barbecue." Noted for his superior musicianship, Armstrong was also an influencial jazz vocalist. Many jazz scholars credit him as the inventor of scat singing, which he introduced in his song "Heebie Jeebies" late in the decade.

The other two major jazz soloists in the 1920s were Sidney Bechet and Coleman Hawkins. Bechet, who grew up in New Orleans, was the first jazz musician to experiment with a soprano saxophone in an ensemble setting. Hawkins' transformed the tenor saxophone into a front-line instrument while playing with Fletcher Henderson's big band in New York. This large dance orchestra showcased the top jazz soloists of the era, like Hawkins and Louis Armstrong. But more important to Henderson was his brilliant young arranger from West Virginia named Don Redman. Together, they established the first golden rule of jazz band arranging: the need for interplay between a brass

and reed section. This principle became the basis for the "swing" band era of the 1930s.

The two most important jazz composers of the decade were Ferdinand "Jelly Roll" Morton and Thomas "Fats" Waller. Morton led his own New Orleans jazz ensemble, the Red Hot Peppers, during much of this period. Together, they recorded some of his best-known compositions, including "Dr. Jazz," "Black Bottom Stomp," and "Jungle Blues." Waller grew up in Harlem listening to the local stride piano professors. By the 1920s, he was a popular entertainer, noted for both his rambunctious piano playing and his light-hearted songs. He wrote much of his own material in collaboration with lyricist Andy Razaf, including some of

In the thirties, Fats Waller made a series of recordings based on classical music, but they were never released because record executives feared that the music would "offend the longhairs."

his biggest hits like "Honeysuckle Rose" and "Ain't Misbehavin'." Waller recorded more than 100 songs during the decade, making him the most popular race record artist in the jazz vocals category.

Blues had more race record releases and sales in the 1920s than jazz and gospel combined. One result of this trend was that a larger sampling of blues from the grassroots was documented for posterity: all of the major rural blues repertoires and styles were commercially recorded during the decade. In addition to the luminaries of rural blues, the race record companies also recorded the first manifestations of an urban blues tradition, as well as the work of women like Ma Rainey, Ida Cox, Bessie Smith, Lovie Austin, and Alberta Hunter, who laid the groundwork for a vaudeville or "classic" blues tradition in urban America.

By the end of the 1920s, black popular song had reached a new plateau. It had finally succeeded in entering the mainstream of American popular music on its own terms. The age of blackface stereotypes and even white cover versions was being eclipsed by a groundswell of authentic gospel, jazz, and blues direct from the cradle of African Ameri-

Whether or not Clarence "Pine-Top" Smith's "Boogie Woogie" was the original is a matter of debate, but this song published in 1929 did start a boogie woogie piano craze that lasted through the 1930s.

can culture. For the first time ever, significant numbers of talented black musicians and songwriters were coming to the forefront of the music industry as innovators and trend setters, if not yet as producers and owners.

This group, spearheaded by Bessie Smith, Louis Armstrong, Ma Rainey, Jelly Roll Morton, Fats Waller, Fletcher Henderson, and Leroy Carr, to name only the most obvious, went on to change the soundscape of commercial music. More specifically, they introduced new black rhythms, melodic formulas, vocal techniques, and instrumental styles into the Tin Pan Alley popular music mix. Simultaneously, the black musical renaissance begun in the 1890s was being absorbed and extended by a new generation of African Americans who came of age in the 1920s and 1930s. Many of them had migrated with their families to the cities, where they learned to make music in the storefront churches and tenderloin cabarets. It was in these black urban ghettos that gospel, jazz, and the blues took on a renewed vigor and sense of urgency as they interacted and ultimately evolved into new urban genres of black popular song.

Ironically, the collapse of the music industry during the Depression allowed these novel urban styles to mature at their own pace and within their own milieu, with few commercial distractions. This distance from the Tin Pan Alley assembly lines and standards proved to be beneficial for the next tidal wave of black popular music to wash over the land in the wake of World War II.

NOBLE SISSLE AND EUBIE BLAKE

Eubie Blake was born James Hubert Blake in Baltimore, Maryland, on February 7, 1883. He played the organ at six years old, got his first job playing in a brothel at 15, and made his professional stage debut in a Pennsylvania medicine show at the age of 18.

In 1905, Blake moved to New York City, where he decided to try to publish his first song, "Sounds of Africa." He asked the influential and fiery Will Marion Cook to accompany him to the publisher, and his song was accepted for $100. However, when Kurt Schindler, the arranger who was going to score it, asked why Blake changed keys without modulation, Blake related: "Cook flared up and said, 'What right have you to question my protegé? How long have you been a Negro?' 'I'm only asking a question,' Schindler said. 'Well you have no right to ask it. We write differently from other people.' 'Good day, gentlemen,' said Schindler, and all bets were off." The song, renamed "Charleston Rag," was not published until after 1919.

Noble Sissle was born in Indianapolis, Indiana, on July 10, 1889. His early interest in music came from his father, a minister and organist. The Sissles moved to Cleveland when Noble was 17, and in 1908, before graduating from high school, he joined a male quartet for a four-week run of the Midwest vaudeville circuit. After graduating, he joined a gospel quartet for a tour on the same circuit.

Riding the wave of new interest in black entertainers brought on by the success of James Reese Europe, Sissle was asked to organize his own orchestra, which he led at Indianapolis' Severin Hotel. In 1915, he left the city for Baltimore.

Sissle and Blake became songwriting partners in 1915 after they met as members of Joe Porter's Serenaders. Their first song was "It's All Your Fault." They got some help in writing it from their friend Eddie Nelson and decided to try it out on Sophie Tucker, who was known to be interested in promoting black songwriters. Tucker liked the song so much that she used it in her act the night after she heard it. "It's All Your Fault" was published in Baltimore, and the partners made $200.

For a while, Sissle and Blake performed separately. In 1916, Sissle was invited to work for James Reese Europe in his Clef Club, and within three or four months, he was leading his own group within the organization. The summer of that year, Blake rejoined him.

When war broke out in 1917, Sissle enlisted with Europe and helped him recruit members for the military band he was forming. Blake, too old for military service at 35, stayed stateside, putting music to songs Sissle and Europe sent back. When the armistice was signed, Europe and Sissle returned, and the three hoped to work together to bring African American theatrical shows back to Broadway. It all came to an abrupt end when Europe was killed by a band member.

Noble Sissle and Eubie Blake.

After Europe's death, Sissle and Blake were encouraged by his manager and the backers of the band to enter the white vaudeville circuit. There were very few black performers besides Sissle and Blake on what was known as the Keith circuit, and never more than one act at the same venue because only one African American act was included in each show. Sissle and Blake, who billed themselves as "The Dixie Duo," were eventually highly successful. Patterned after their Clef Club presentations, their act was performed without blackface and with an on-stage piano as their only prop. Their many hit songs in vaudeville included "Gee, I'm Glad I'm from Dixie," their opening number.

Sissle and Blake met the men with whom they were to make history at a NAACP benefit in Philadelphia in 1920. Flournoy Miller and Aubrey Lyles were veterans in black show business who had written and starred in productions since 1910. Miller believed that the only way African American performers would make it back into white theaters with any dignity was through musical comedy, and after Sissle and Blake's performance, he and Lyles approached the pair to ask if they would be interested in teaming together for such a production. Sissle and Blake, who saw this as a way to achieve Europe's dream as well as their own, agreed. So the four men put together their resources and set about to write, direct, manage, and star in their own musical comedy.

Shuffle Along was patterned after the African American shows presented during the first few years of the century, and when a casting call was issued, a number of performers from those early shows turned out. The partners found a backer, and after a shaky road show tour, *Shuffle Along* opened in New York on May 23, 1921.

Though many barriers to the free expression of African American creativity had been broken down by this time, a very important taboo remained: serious romantic love between black characters was seldom shown on stage. According to James Weldon Johnson, who had confronted the same problem at the turn of the century, "If anything approaching a love duet was introduced in a musical comedy, it had to be broadly burlesqued. The reason behind this…lay in the belief that a love scene between two Negroes could not strike a white audience except as ridiculous."

When the romantic song "Love Will Find a Way" premiered, Blake was on stage playing piano for the actors, but his partners were at the stage door ready to flee if the theater erupted in violence. Instead, the song ended to great applause, and another wall came tumbling down.

Another ground-breaking aspect of *Shuffle Along* lay in the seating arrangements for its performances: for the first time, blacks sat in sections previously reserved for whites only. Nevertheless, there were still separate sections for the two races; the balcony section, often referred to as "Nigger Heaven," was still for blacks only. Some artistic concessions were still made to the racist assumptions of the time. Band members memorized the score and performed without sheet music because, as Blake explained, "people didn't believe that black people could read music—they wanted to think that our ability was just natural talent."

The most popular song to come out of the show was originally written as a waltz, but Lottie Gee, the young singer who was to perform it, complained that she couldn't sing it in waltz time, and the uptempo "I'm Just Wild about Harry" became a hit. The dancing in *Shuffle Along* so impressed Florenz Ziegfeld and George White that they both hired women from its cast to teach dance steps to the white women in their respective productions.

Shuffle Along was the first all-black musical to become a box office hit, and it started a resurgence of African American shows. Following the show's successful run and subsequent successful road tours, however, the team that created it ended their professional association.

Soon after, Sissle and Blake wrote a dozen songs for a new white musical, *Elsie*. The duo then made an early sound-on-film recording. In 1924, Sissle and Blake tried their hand at another production, *In Bamville*, which was eventually renamed *Chocolate Dandies*. However, according to David Ewen, the show failed because it didn't fit the stereotype of "fast dancing and Negroid humor."

In 1925, Sissle and Blake toured Europe. While abroad, they wrote songs for a British revue and began to have disagreements about the direction of their work: Blake wanted to return to America, and Sissle wanted to stay in Europe. Although they returned to the States, Sissle went back to Europe soon afterwards, and the team broke up.

In the thirties, Sissle put together a successful orchestra, and Blake worked with various African American songwriters including Henry Creamer and Andy Razaf. He even wrote a song that was used for a Pabst Beer commercial. In 1933, Sissle, Blake, and Flournoy Miller attempted an unsuccessful revival of *Shuffle Along*.

Later in life, Sissle became involved in the Negro Actor's Guild which he helped found, serving as its first president. In 1968, he and Blake recorded together on an album entitled "86 Years of Eubie Blake." Noble Sissle died on December 17, 1975. Blake lived on to be 100, playing piano and entertaining until the very end, which came on February 12, 1983.

ARTIST PROFILE
CECIL MACK

Richard C. McPherson, better known as Cecil Mack, was born in Norfolk, Virginia, in 1883. He was educated at the Norfolk Mission School and attended Lincoln University in Pennsylvania but failed to graduate due to lack of funds. He also attended the University of Pennsylvania Medical School for one semester.

In 1901, Mack wrote the lyrics to "Good Morning, Carrie." Its sheet music cover featured Bert Williams and George Walker, who sang it on their historic recordings for the Victor Talking Machine Company. By 1904, Mack had written lyrics for more songs including "The Little Gypsy Maid" for the play, *The Wild Rose*, and "Zono, My Congo Queen." In that year, he wrote his first big hit, "Teasing," with Harry Von Tilzer, a white New York songwriter and publisher.

Early in 1905, Mack organized the Gotham Music Publishing Company. Actual ownership of the company is unknown. In its four months of existence, the majority of its songs were composed by African Americans including Will Marion Cook, James Reese Europe, and Mack himself.

About this time another New York firm,

the Attucks Music Publishing Company, was formed, taking its name from Crispus Attucks, the first black killed in the American Revolution. This company's catalog was also dominated by the works of blacks, among them Alex Rogers, Jesse Shipp, Chris Smith, and Bert Williams, and many of its covers featured pictures of Williams and Walker. In less than a year, the company issued about 20 songs.

On May 29, 1905, Cecil Mack was part of a group that founded the Gotham-Attucks Music Publishing Company, a merger of the two companies. Again, while the ownership of this company is unknown, in July of 1906, the *New York Age* referred to McPherson as Gotham-Attucks' "secretary and treasurer and general business director." Whether Cecil Mack was the sole owner or was in partnership with other black musicians and songwriters, this was likely the first African American-owned publishing company in New York. In its six years of existence, before it was bought by Ferdinand E. Mierisch in 1911, Gotham-Attucks performed a vital service to the black music scene.

"The House of Melody," as Gotham-Attucks was also known, published the music from two of the famous Williams and Walker musicals, *In Abyssinia* and *Bandana Land*. The covers of their sheet music broke new ground in that they did not resort to the racial stereotyping used by other companies, and the few coon songs included in their catalog were never labeled as such. However, after 1908, for unknown reasons most of the black songwriters except for Mack and Chris Smith left the company.

Cecil Mack wrote the lyrics for many songs between 1907 and 1910. His "I'm Miss Hanna From Savannah" was written exclusively for Ada Overton Walker, George Walker's wife. He composed the lyrics to James Reese Europe's music for *The Black Politician*, produced in 1907 for the Smart Set Company, a musical-comedy touring company formed by Ernest Hogan and minstrel Billy McLain that served as a training ground for many black songsters and musicians.

In 1910, Gotham-Attucks published a song used by Ada Walker in another famous African American road show called "His Honor the Barber." The name of the song with words by Mack and music by Ford Dabney was "That's Why They Call Me Shine," and it became famous. Now simply known as "Shine," the tune was redone with success years later by Louis Armstrong, Ella Fitzgerald, and Ry Cooder. According to Perry Bradford, himself a songster and publisher, the song was written about an actual man named Shine who was with George Walker when they were badly beaten during the New York City race riot of 1900. In his thinly veiled work of fiction published in 1912, *The Auto-Biography of an Ex-Colored Man*, James Weldon Johnson included a character called Shine who was probably based upon the same individual.

Cecil Mack's most famous work became a

Cecil Mack.

musical hallmark of the twenties. It is a song that everyone danced to, that made a lot of money, and that will never be forgotten. But ironically enough for its lyricist, it is a song that no one remembers the words to—the "Charleston."

The "Charleston" was composed in 1913 by African American James P. Johnson, who played it at dances for black longshoremen recently moved from South Carolina. Johnson was the master and originator of a style of piano playing known as "stride." He had also written some instrumentals during the teens, including the "Steeplechase Rag" and the "Twilight Rag." In 1923, after the success of *Shuffle Along*, when Flournoy Miller and Aubrey Lyles, two comedians who had shared in that production's prosperity, decided to put together a new show, they asked Johnson and Cecil Mack to provide the songs.

The name of Miller and Lyles' show was

Runnin' Wild, and the "Charleston" was one of the songs performed. Soon after the show opened, America went Charleston crazy. *Variety* reported that "in Boston's Pickwick Club, a tenderloin dance hall, the vibrations of Charleston dancers caused the place to collapse, killing fifty." The *New York Times* reported in 1925 that the dance was so popular one criterion in hiring black domestic workers was that they be able to teach the dance to their white employers. James Weldon Johnson wrote that when the dance was introduced in the play, the performers:

> *did not depend wholly on the orchestra—an extraordinary jazz band—but had the major part of the chorus supplement it with hand and foot patting. The effect was electrical and contagious. It was the best demonstration of beating out complex rhythms I have ever witnessed; and, I do not believe New York ever before witnessed anything of just its sort.*

It is fortunate that the songs from *Runnin' Wild* were performed at all, as there were some financial differences between the songwriters and Miller and Lyles. According to Perry Bradford, Johnson and Mack had tied up the show in Pittsburgh with "a royalty accounting rope."

Mack became a member of ASCAP within the first ten years of its existence. This was not an easy task for an African American composer.

Harry T. Burleigh and James Weldon Johnson had been charter members, but it took 12 years before another eight black musicians and lyricists, including W. C. Handy, Will Marion Cook, and Maceo Pinkard, were invited into this exclusive profit-sharing club. The prerequisites were strict, and only the most established artists could afford to become members.

In 1925, Cecil Mack, Jesse Shipp, and James P. Johnson wrote the book for *Mooching Along*. Mack also formed Cecil Mack's Southland Singers who were used in *Bombolla* four years later.

The success of *Shuffle Along, Runnin' Wild*, and other shows of the period finally broke down the barriers that had kept black productions from prospering. The shows were popular not only in New York but also on the road, and with their popularity came profit. Doors opened for more African American performances as well as for such African American shows produced by whites as Lew Leslie's outstanding *Blackbirds* series, in which Mack's Cecil Mack's Choir made its debut.

In 1931, his choir performed in Lew Leslie's *Rhapsody in Black*. Along with George Gershwin, Rosamond Johnson, Dorothy Fields, Jimmy McHugh, and W. C. Handy, he also wrote lyrics and music for the show. The versatile Mack did the vocal arrangements for its spirituals and folk songs as well. Richard C. McPherson died in New York in 1944.

W.C. HANDY

William Christopher Handy, the "Father of the Blues," was born in Florence, Alabama, on November 16, 1873. Both his father and grandfather were ministers. He got his first lessons on the cornet in a barber shop, not an unusual spot for music lessons at the time. Handy taught school before he was 19, but then left home to work in a factory in Bessemer, Alabama, because it paid more. Around 1893, he organized a quartet that performed at the Chicago World's Fair, an exposition which attracted a large number of musicians, including many rag-playing pianists like Tom Turpin and Scott Joplin.

After the fair, Handy traveled the country, trying to make a career in music. For a time, he taught music at A & M College in Huntsville, Alabama. However, he was not satisfied with teaching and left to join Mahara's Minstrels as a cornetist, eventually becoming leader of the troupe. While with Mahara's, he traveled extensively and even performed in Cuba. Handy's nickname from these days was "Fess." Usually short for "professor," it suggests the respect other musicians had for his musical knowledge.

In 1902, Handy formed his own band in Clarksville, Mississippi. This group was as much a marching band as a dance orchestra, and they performed for whites and blacks alike. At one of the performances for a white audience, Handy was asked to "play some of your own music." When he began to play, the audience loudly protested that he was not honoring their request.

He and his group were asked to step aside. Then three local black men came on stage with string instruments and performed a type of primitive blues. It was obvious to Handy from the crowd reaction that he had missed something in his musical education: the rural sounds had both musical merit and crowd-pleasing potential. It was a lesson that would change Handy's life.

Handy's strengths as an artist were his strong musical background and his ability to remember any song he heard. The roots of the blues he created lay in black folk songs, and he freely acknowledged these origins. In an interview, he said:

Each one of my blues is based on some old Negro song of the South….Something that sticks in my mind, that I hum to myself when I'm not thinking about it. Some old song that is a part of the memories of my childhood and of my race. I can tell you the exact song I used as a basis for any one of my blues.

In 1909, Handy and his band were asked to play for the campaign of the Memphis political boss, Edward H. Crump. At the time, the most popular song in their repertoire was a piece called "Mr. Crump" which contained some lines not exactly complimentary to their patron:

*Mr. Crump doan allow no easy
    riders here.*

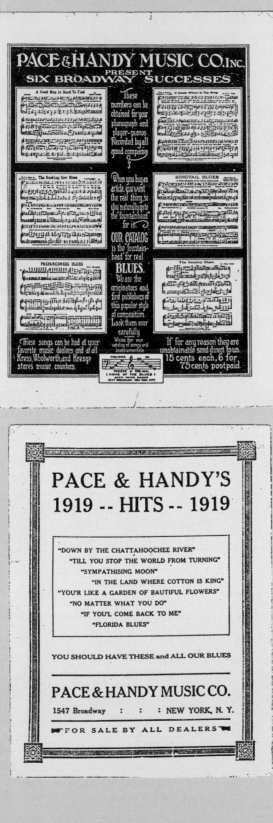

*We doan care what Mr. Crump
      doan allow,
We gonna Barrel-house anyhow.
Mr. Crump can go and catch
      himself some air.*

But Boss Crump was not interested in the lyrics if he ever even heard them. What he was interested in was the drawing power of Handy's music, which proved so successful that Crump won the election. Later new words by George Norton were added, and the title was changed to "The Memphis Blues."

It was the first blues Handy ever wrote. Many consider it to be the first blues song in history, although due to Handy's problems finding a publisher it was preceded in print by "Baby Seals Blues" by Artie Matthews in August of 1912 and the "Dallas Blues" by Hart A. Wand in September of the same year. Handy's song, which had been released as an instrumental in 1910, came out at the end of September or the beginning of October 1912, when Handy finally decided to publish it himself.

Selling the song to retailers was not much easier than selling it to a publisher, and one major white music retailer flatly refused to purchase Handy's work. Handy wrote in his autobiography, *Father of the Blues*:

At the time I approached him his windows were displaying "At the Ball" by J. Lubrie Hill,

118

a colored composer who had gone to New York from Memphis some time earlier. Around it were grouped copies of recent successes by such Negro composers as Cole and Johnson, Scott Joplin, and the Williams and Walker musical comedies. So when he suggested that his trade wouldn't stand for his selling my work, I pointed out as tactfully as I could that the majority of his musical hits of the moment had come from the Gotham-Attucks Co., a firm of Negro publishers in New York. I'll never forget his smile. "Yes," he said pleasantly. "I know that—but my customers don't."

W. C. Handy.

Racial prejudice was clearly a factor in making Handy's songs difficult to sell, but so too was the blues' unfamiliarity to most mainstream music publishers. However, this same characteristic also worked to the music's advantage by keeping it from being watered down by Tin Pan Alley. Any composer could take the title "blues" and turn it into something it wasn't, but most found it hard to write in the real blues style.

"The Memphis Blues" quickly became popular throughout the country. Florenz Ziegfeld liked the song so much that he later told Handy he gave a party every time he heard it. Black composer Will Vodery told Handy that he was personally responsible for putting five black bands on Broadway—the peculiarities of the song made it too difficult for white musicians to interpret.

According to Noble Sissle, "The Memphis Blues" inspired the fox trot, created by Vernon and Irene Castle. They were one of the most famous ballroom dance teams of the day, and their musical director was James Reese Europe. Most of their material was fast paced, but during intermissions, while the Castles caught their breath, Europe played "The Memphis Blues" at a slow tempo. He did this regularly, and the

Castles became fascinated by the song's rhythm. When Europe suggested that they originate a slow dance adapted to it, the Castles liked the idea, and the new dance, introduced as the "Bunny Hug," was soon after renamed the "Fox Trot."

Another early song by Handy was the "Beale Street Blues," named for what he said was "the colored thoroughfare in Memphis" where you could "find the best and worst of the Negro life." According to Handy, the song was inspired by a fellow musician:

As I was walking down Beale Street one night, my attention was caught by the sound of a piano. The insistent Negro rhythms were broken by a tinkle in the treble, then by a rumble in the bass; then they came together. I entered the cheap cafe and found a colored man at the piano, dog tired. He told me he had to play from seven at night until seven in the morning, and rested himself with alternate hands. He told me of his life, and it seemed to me that this poor, tired, happy-go-lucky musician represented his race. I set it down in notes, keeping faith with all that made the background of that poor piano thumper.

While in Memphis, Handy also wrote the "St. Louis Blues," which proved to be his best-selling number and one of the most recorded songs in the history of music. Its popularity was not confined to the United States: England's King Edward VIII once asked Scottish bagpipers to play it for him, and in the thirties, when Ethiopia was invaded by Italy, it became the Ethiopian battle hymn. Forty years after it was first published, it was still supplying Handy with annual royalties of nearly $25,000.

After mild success with his Memphis-based publishing firm, Handy and his partner, Harry Pace, decided to move their operation to New York City, where they started publishing in 1917. During the twenties, Handy continued to write songs, and in 1926, he wrote *Blues: An Anthology*, which contained many of his earlier compositions and explained their origins.

During the thirties, Handy composed a number of spirituals, and in 1938 he published a book entitled *W. C. Handy's Collection of Negro Spirituals*. Later that year, he was given a tribute at Carnegie Hall. In 1939, at the New York World's Fair, he was listed as a leading contributor to American culture. W. C. Handy died in New York City on March 28, 1958. In 1969, he was honored posthumously by the United States Postal Service with a commemorative stamp. A part of the Beale Street area of Memphis is known today as W. C. Handy Park.

CLARENCE WILLIAMS

Clarence Williams was both an artist and an entrepreneur. Highly energetic and adept at all sides of the music business from writing, publishing, and performing to managing other artists, he worked with the most famous early female blues singer, Bessie Smith. The songs he wrote were popular across the United States; some of his compositions in the Dixieland style have become classics.

Williams was born on the outskirts of New Orleans, in Plaquemine, Louisiana, on October 8, 1898. He was of Choctaw Indian and Creole heritage. His father was a bass player who made his living as a hotel owner, and as a child, Williams began his musical education performing in the family hotel and singing in the streets. When he was 12, he left home and joined Billy Kersands' famous minstrel show as a singer. Shortly thereafter, he became the troupe's master of ceremonies.

On Williams' return to New Orleans, he started a suit-cleaning service for the many style-conscious piano professors in that city. He also began playing piano in the honky-tonks of New Orleans' Storyville. In this legendary red-light district, Williams, a man not noted for his modesty, admitted that he was overshadowed by Tony Jackson, the influential rag pianist who wrote "Pretty Baby." Williams also played professionally with Sidney Bechet and Bunk Johnson, two future jazz stars.

He invested much of his time in learning new material, even writing to New York for the latest songs. During this period, he also managed his own cabaret, and wrote his first money-making composition, "Brownskin, Who You For?," recorded on Columbia Records. The $1,600 check he received for it in 1916 was, according to Williams, the most money anyone in New Orleans had ever made for a song.

Around 1915, he and Armand Piron started a New Orleans-based publishing company, which was in business for several years. Piron was a band leader whose most famous composition was "I Wish I Could Shimmy Like My Sister Kate." In 1917, he and Williams put together a vaudeville act, and they achieved moderate success with Piron on the fiddle and Williams on the piano and singing.

While touring, they became acquainted with W. C. Handy, who helped them place some of their compositions in Memphis music stores. When an important concert in Atlanta was moved from a black auditorium to a white one because so many whites wanted to attend, Handy asked Williams and Piron to join him to strengthen the program. The concert was a triumph, and the New Orleans duo stopped the show.

About this time, Williams claimed to be the first songwriter to use the word "jazz" on a piece of sheet music, and his business card began touting him as "The Originator of Jazz and Boogie Woogie." Williams' writing partner on some songs during the late teens was Spencer

Clarence Williams.

more, and Williams' entrepreneurial skills enabled him to profit from this next phase in the entertainment business: selling recordings of black female blues singers.

In 1921, Williams married Eva Taylor. She was one of the first female singers heard on the radio, and her performances and style influenced many future vocal stars. Among the songs she and her husband collaborated on and performed together was "May We Meet Again," written "in memory of our beloved Florence Mills," one of the most popular black stage entertainers of the time.

Williams understood the potential selling-power of New Orleans music in the North, and since New York City was the center of the music publishing business, he sold his Chicago music stores in 1923 and moved there. He rented space in the Gaiety Theater Building at 1547 Broadway, which was already established as an office building for other African American entertainers including Bert Williams, Will Vodery, Pace and Handy, and Perry Bradford, and in February of that year, he and Bessie Smith went to Columbia to record her first sides.

The first two releases featured Smith accompanied by Williams on piano; one, "Gulf Coast Blues," was even composed by Williams and published by his company. Williams accompanied Smith on many of the songs she recorded during that highly productive year and claimed writer's credit on such numbers as "Baby, Won't

Williams (no relation). Their "Royal Garden Blues" became a Dixieland classic.

Anticipating the exodus of talent from New Orleans to the northern cities spurred on by the closing of Storyville, Williams moved to Chicago in 1920. The music store he opened near the Vendome Theater proved so lucrative that he eventually owned three music stores in the city, but Williams did not confine his energies to mere proprietorship. Nineteen-twenty was the year Mamie Smith recorded Perry Bradford's "Crazy Blues" and "It's Right Here for You." When the public got their first hearing of a black woman's voice singing the blues, they wanted

You Please Come Home" and "T'ain't Nobody's Bizness If I Do." It should be noted, however, that Williams had a reputation for claiming credit for works he did not compose entirely on his own, and the origins of many of these songs remain in question.

He was also less than honest with the singer. He convinced Smith that she was under contract to Columbia. In reality, she had signed a contract naming him as her manager, and he was pocketing half of her recording fee. This episode came to a swift conclusion when Smith and a boyfriend made a surprise trip to Williams' office, demanding that she be released from that obligation and allowed to sign directly with Columbia.

Not all of his activities were so self-serving. Willie "The Lion" Smith, who claimed that Williams was the first New Orleans musician to influence jazz in New York, also credited Williams with helping other African American songwriters like himself, James P. Johnson, and Fats Waller. From 1923 to 1928, Williams was the artist and repertoire director for Okeh Records, and from this powerful position he was able to seek out and develop new talent. During this time, he organized numerous sessions which advanced the careers of many early jazz greats such as Louis Armstrong and Sidney Bechet. He also employed a number of other jazz musicians including Don Redman, King Oliver, and Coleman Hawkins.

A shrewd businessman, Williams was in a position to help new artists in many ways. He could arrange their recording sessions, supply their material, publish their compositions, and manage their business affairs. Like others in his profession, he was also capable of taking advantage of the unknowing performer, and did so fairly regularly.

Between 1923 and 1937, Williams proved to be a prolific producer, organizing at least two recording sessions a month and recording more than 300 sides under his own name. It was common for him to record with one company and, if he didn't like the results, go across town and record the same session for another company under a different name. The Dixie Washboard Band and Bluegrass Footwarmers are but two of the pseudonyms he used in his pursuit of the best possible session.

In 1927, Williams tried his hand at musical theater. He wrote the book and music for and also produced the show *Bottomland*, which starred his wife, Eva Taylor. The show was not a critical success. However, Williams' New York publishing company prospered, continuing to do business until 1943 when he sold its catalog of more than 2,000 songs to Decca for a reputed $50,000.

From the late thirties until he lost his sight after being hit by a cab in 1956, Clarence Williams spent most of his time composing. He died in Queens, New York, on November 6, 1965.

"MOOD INDIGO"

The Depression reversed the fortunes of the entire music industry. Both the TOBA and the race record labels suffered devastating financial setbacks. By 1927, the TOBA had begun to falter, unable to compete with commercial radio and especially talking motion pictures. After the stock market crash of 1929, it went out of business, leaving hundreds of black performers without jobs, and a smaller number of vaudeville theater owners in need of a new source of entertainment and income. Individual TOBA-affiliated theaters were left to fend for themselves as best they could, a situation which tended to benefit local black talent who were more likely to get hired under these new circumstances.

In the record business, sales fell from more than $100 million in 1927 to $6 million in 1933. Consequently, race record releases were drastically cut back, field recording forays into the South were discontinued, the labels manufactured fewer and fewer copies of each title, and record prices fell from 75 to 35 cents per disc. Where the average race record on the market sold about 10,000 copies in the mid-1920s, the figure plummeted to 2,000 in 1930, and bottomed out at 400 copies in 1932.

Most of the race record labels were either gradually forced out of business or purchased by more prosperous media corporations based in radio and film. During the Depression, RCA took over the Victor Record Company; Majestic Radio Corporation acquired the Columbia Record Company for a short period of time; and Warner Brothers Pictures got into the business briefly when it bought up the Brunswick label. Later, Warner sold Brunswick to Consolidated Film Industries, which also acquired the Vocalion label. Finally, the Columbia Broadcasting System (CBS) purchased the Columbia Record Company, then later the Vocalion catalog. The record companies which shut down their race label operations during the economic downturn were Paramount, Okeh, and Gennett. As early as 1933, the race record business, like the TOBA, was a fatality of the Depression.

The popular music that defined the 1930s as the Swing Era in spite of hard times evolved from the black jazz bands of the previous decade. In particular, the ingenuous arrangements of Don Redman with the Fletcher Henderson orchestra became the prototype for the large jazz ensembles of the Depression years. By then, a number of important African American swing bands had taken up where Redman and Henderson's group left off.

No doubt, the two most creative African American swing bands of the decade were those led by Edward "Duke" Ellington and William "Count" Basie. In the 1920s, Duke Ellington was just starting out as a novice bandleader, arranger, and composer in New York, after moving there from Washington, D.C., his hometown. His major influence during these formative years were Clef Club veterans Will Marion Cook, who taught him how to compose jazz melodies, and Will Vodery.

In 1925, Ellington was spotted by an en-

Edward Kennedy "Duke" Ellington was born in Washington, D.C., in 1899. In the late twenties, his orchestra and their trademark "jungle music" were all the rage at the Cotton Club. The "jungle music" effect was achieved by using mutes in the horns to imitate animal growls and roars. In 1931, Ellington wrote "Mood Indigo," the first of his famous mood compositions, with help from band member Albany "Barney" Bigard.

terprising young white music publisher and booking agent named Irving Mills. He agreed to manage Ellington and his band in exchange for 45 percent of the profits, an outrageous though not unusual figure in the early years of the race music business.

To his credit, Mills opened certain music industry doors that were most often closed to African Americans. He negotiated a record deal with the Columbia label, and he got Ellington and his band booked into the Cotton Club for what developed into a five-year run. The Cotton Club showcased black entertainers for a rich white clientele, hence the pay was better than the group had been making, even after Mills' cut. More important, their extended en-

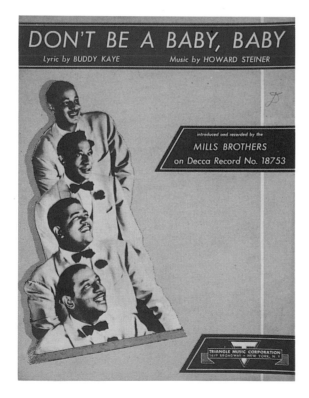

The Mills Brothers, who were, unlike many similarly named groups, really brothers, were the most popular vocal group in history. Their father, John, Sr., joined the group in 1935 on the death of his son, John, Jr.

gagement gave Ellington the time and space he needed to develop his talent for composition and his band's unique tonal approach to swing music.

For his part in the Duke Ellington success story, Irving Mills was paid handsomely; he went on to become a major force in the music business. While working with Ellington, Mills saw fit to add his name to the copyright on Ellington's songs. As a result, he got both equal credit and royalties from tunes like "The Mooch" and "Mood Indigo." After 14 years of artistic and financial success, Duke Ellington severed his business ties to Irving Mills and Columbia Records. Once the break was made, he never spoke about the subject in public. Over the next four decades, Ellington continued to compose an impressive range of music, thus solidifying his reputation as a jazz giant and one of this country's greatest twentieth-century composers.

While Ellington was in the forefront of swing band music on the East Coast in the 1930s, Count Basie's aggregation from Kansas City achieved fame as the Southwest's leading exponent of swing. In this case, swing was characterized by a unique fusion of regional jazz and blues styles. Basie was from New Jersey, but he spent the formative years of his career as a jazz pianist and then bandleader in the Southwest. He joined the Blue Devils out of Oklahoma City in the late 1920s, and then moved on to Bennie Moten's band based in Kansas City, which he eventually took over after Moten's death. Basie's band showcased some of the finest jazzmen in the country, musicians like bassist Walter Page, trombonist/guitarist Eddie Durham, trumpeter Oran "Hot Lips" Page, blues "shouter" Jimmy Rushing, and saxophonists Ben Webster and Lester "Pres" Young.

The new upsurge in black popular song, established irreversibly in the 1920s and grounded in gospel, jazz, and the blues, continued to flourish at the grassroots throughout the Depression years. During this period, new gospel quartets like the Dixie Hummingbirds and the Soul Stirrers emerged as did female gospel singers like Mahalia Jackson, Roberta Martin, and Clara Ward. The gospel quartets inspired their secular counterparts, like the Ink Spots and the Mills Brothers, who were popular with both black and white audiences even prior to World War II. Jazz vocalists like Fats Waller and increasingly, Louis Armstrong, continued to enjoy great acclaim, as did newcomers Ella Fitzgerald and Billie Holiday. The blues both secured an urban foothold and remained popular in the rural South.

It is indisputable that African Americans were exploited by the race record business in the years preceding World War II. They were paid lower wages than their white counterparts, they were cheated out of their copyright royalties, and they were forced to water down their music. Nevertheless, black performers seized this opportunity to document much of their music for posterity. While using the recording industry as a means of extending their musical culture, they also began to make visible inroads into the mainstream of American popular song.

This is but one of many song folios released during the thirties and forties that featured the works of jazz musicians.

During this era, close to 15,000 race records were released, of which approximately 10,000 were blues titles, 3,000 were jazz titles, and 2,000 were gospel titles. Thousands of African American musicians, both folk and professional, made contributions to this bonanza of audio evidence documenting their feelings, experiences, and struggles. Millions of African Americans purchased race records for home entertainment. Along with local live music venues, race records and phonographs were at the center of black social life in the urban ghettos. They would play a pivotal role in diversifying and invigorating black popular song in the years ahead, which in turn would continue to enrich American popular music in general.

SOURCES

Albertson, Chris. *Bessie*. New York: Scarborough House, 1974.

Albertson, Chris. Notes to "Bessie Smith: The Complete Recordings Vol. 1." Columbia Legacy C2K 47091.

Barlow, William. *Looking Up At Down: The Emergence of Blues Culture*. Philadelphia: Temple University Press, 1989.

Blesh, Rudi and Harriet Janis. *They All Played Ragtime: The True Story of an American Music*. New York: Alfred A. Knopf, 1950.

Blesh, Rudi. *Combo: USA*. Philadelphia: Chilton Book Company, 1971.

Bradford, Perry. *Born With The Blues*. New York: Oak Publications, 1965.

Burton, Jack. *The Blue Book of Tin Pan Alley Vol. 1*. Watkins Glen, N.Y.: Century House Publishing, 1951.

Carr, Ian, Digby Fairweather, and Brian Priestley. *Jazz: The Essential Companion*. London: Grafton Books, 1987.

Charters, Ann. *Nobody: The Story of Bert Williams*. New York: Da Capo Press, 1983.

Chilton, John. *Who's Who of Jazz*. New York: Da Capo Press, 1985.

Clarke, Donald. *The Penguin Encyclopedia of Popular Music*. London: Penguin Books, 1989.

Collier, James Lincoln. *The Making of Jazz: A Comprehensive History*. New York: Dell Publishing Company, 1978.

Cook, Will Marion, *Theater Arts* (Sept. 1947). In *Readings in Black American Music* compiled and edited by Eileen Southern, New York: W. W. Norton & Company, 1971.

Ellington, Duke. *Music is My Mistress*. New York: Doubleday & Company, 1973.

Epstein, Dena J. *Sinful Tunes and Spirituals: Black Folk Music to the Civil War*. Urbana, Ill.: University of Illinois Press, 1977.

Europe, James Reese, *Literary Digest* (April 26, 1919). In *Readings in Black American Music* compiled and edited by Eileen Southern, New York: W. W. Norton & Company, 1971.

Ewen, David. *All The Years of American Popular Music*. Englewood Cliffs, N.J.: Prentice Hall, 1977.

Fletcher, Tom. *The Tom Fletcher Story: One Hundred Years of the Negro in Show Business*. New York: Da Capo Press, 1984.

Gilbert, Douglas. *American Vaudeville: Its Life and Times*. New York: Dover Publications, 1963.

Hamm, Charles. *Yesterdays: Popular Song in America*. New York: W.W. Norton & Company, 1983.

Handy, W. C., *Etude Music Magazine* (March 1940). In *Readings in Black American Music* compiled and edited by Eileen Southern, New York: W.W. Norton & Company 1971.

Handy, W. C. *Father of the Blues: An Autobiography*. New York: Macmillan Publishing Company, 1941.

Harrison, Daphne Duval. *Black Pearls: Blues Queens of the 1920s*. New Brunswick, N.J.: Rutgers University Press, 1988.

Higham, Charles. *Ziegfeld*. Chicago: Regnery Gateway, 1972.

Johnson, James Weldon. *Along This Way*. New York: Viking Press, 1933.

Johnson, James Weldon. *Black Manhattan*. New York: Alfred A. Knopf, 1930.

Johnson, James Weldon. *The Book of American Negro Spirituals*. New York: Viking Press, 1925.

Kimball, Robert and William Bolcom. *Reminiscing With Sissle and Blake*. New York: Viking Press, 1973.

Lomax, Alan. *Mister Jelly Roll*. Berkeley: University of California Press, 1950.

Marks, Edward B. *They All Sang: From Tony Pastor to Rudy Vallee*. New York: Viking Press, 1935.

Oliver, Paul, Max Harrison, and William Bolcom. *The New Grove Gospel, Blues and Jazz*. New York: W.W. Norton & Company, 1980.

Ovington, Mary White. *Half A Man*. New York: Longsman, Green & Company, 1911.

Rose, Al. *Eubie Blake*. New York: Macmillan Publishing Company, 1979.

Sampson, Henry T. *Blacks in Blackface: A Source Book on Early Musical Shows*. Metuchen, N.J.: Scarecrow Press, 1980.

Scarborough, Dorothy. *On The Trail of Negro Folksongs*. Cambridge: Harvard University Press, 1925.

Schoener, Allon. *Harlem On My Mind*. New York: Random House, 1968.

Shaw, Arnold. *Black Popular Music in America: From the Spirituals, Minstrels and Ragtime To Soul, Disco, and Hip-Hop*. New York: E. C. Schirmer Music Company, 1986.

Shirley, Wayne D. "The House of Melody: A List of Publications of the Gotham-Attucks Music Publishing Company at the Library of Congress," *The Black Perspective in Music* Vol 15: Spring, 1987, Columbia Heights, N.Y.

Southern, Eileen. *The Music of Black Americans*. New York: W.W. Norton & Company, 1971.

Southern, Eileen, comp. and ed. *Readings in Black American Music*. New York: W. W. Norton & Company, 1971.

Stein, Charles, ed. *American Vaudeville—As Seen by Its Contemporaries*. New York: Alfred A. Knopf, 1984.

Toll, Robert. *Blacking Up: The Minstrel Show in 19th Century America*. New York: Oxford University Press, 1974.

Waldo, Terry. *This is Ragtime*. New York: Da Capo Press, 1976.

Wilder, Alec. *American Popular Song: The Great Innovators, 1900-1950*. New York: Oxford University Press, 1972.

Williams, Bert, "The Comic Side of Trouble," *American Magazine* 85 (January 1918) found in *American Vaudeville As Seen by Its Contemporaries* edited by Charles Stein, New York: Alfred A. Knopf, 1984.

Witmark, Isidore and Isaac Goldberg. *The Story of the House of Witmark: From Ragtime to Swingtime*. New York: Da Capo Press, 1976.

Woll, Allen. *Black Musical Theater: From Coontown to Dreamgirls*. Baton Rouge: Louisiana State University Press, 1989.

INDEX

ARTISTS AND PRODUCERS